THE
FAITH FACTOR

Life in a New Dimension

THE FAITH FACTOR

Life in a New Dimension

VICTOR DUNSTAN

MEGIDDO PRESS
Cardiff

Copyright © Victor Dunstan
Mediddo Press, Cardiff, Wales

First British Casebound Edition 1989
This Revised Edition 1992

All rights reserved.
No part of this publication may be reproduced or
transmitted in any form or by any means, electronic or
mechanical, including photocopy, recording, or any
information storage retrieval system, without permission
in writing from the publisher.

ISBN 0 946922 85 3

Bible quotations are from the Authorised Version
Crown copyright.

Produced and Printed in England for
MEGIDDO PRESS
Grosvenor House, 20 St Andrews Crescent, Cardiff CF1 3DD
by
NUPRINT LTD, Station Road, Harpenden, Herts AL5 4SE

This book is dedicated to my parents
CUTHBERT VICTOR DUNSTAN and
MARY JANE DUNSTAN
who showed me and many others the way
and who are now with Christ.
Also to our good friend Principal George
Jeffreys who pointed THEM, and
multitudes, to that life in the new
dimension.

Contents

	Introduction by The Right Hon. Viscount Tonypandy	9
	Foreword	11
1	'There must be more to life than this!'	17
2	Why the 'you' in you will never die	26
3	You have a problem!	46
4	The faith factor	54
5	The Invisible God	66
6	Whosoever will may come	86
7	A promise from God to you	100
8	What Jesus meant by believing	128
9	Born into the new dimension	135
10	Generation—Degeneration—Regeneration	149
11	The Coming of the Saviour	178
12	God the Father, Son and Holy Spirit	202
13	Creation or Evolution?	216
14	The relationship between faith and behaviour	234
15	It's decision time!	243

Introduction

BY

THE RIGHT HON. VISCOUNT TONYPANDY
FORMER SPEAKER OF THE HOUSE OF COMMONS

Victor Dunstan is a modern day prophet. His perception of God's Word is staggering. In this powerful proclamation of 'The Faith Factor' his confidence reveals his own faith. It is a faith I rejoice to share.

John Wesley's first sermon after his personal experience of Christ was based on the text 'By Grace Are Ye Saved Through Faith'. 'The Faith Factor' is matched by the 'Grace Factor'.

The mercy of God knows no bounds. As Victor Dunstan reminds us in this book the sudden awareness of God's saving power is experienced by people in every walk of life. God is no respecter of persons.

We can never know the mind of God, except to the extent that Jesus has revealed to us the nature of God.

Christian believers experience the love of God time and again, but there is no more mighty proof of His love than the way in which by an act of simple faith on our part, He reveals Himself.

> Only believe, and thou shalt see
> That Christ is all in all to thee.

In this age of doubt and half belief, Victor Dunstan's clarion message is a tonic. I hope that it will be widely read, for I am satisfied that God almighty has inspired him in its writing.

Foreword

There are two things I wish!

I wish I could claim to know *all* about God, but I can't make that claim—and nobody can!

Then I wish I could put myself forward as an example for you to follow and tell you that if you follow me you will not go far wrong, but I can't make *that* claim either—and nobody can!

What I *can* tell you is that I have had an experience—undoubtedly the most exceptional and profound experience of my life—in which God initiated me into a *new dimension* of life when He imparted to me *the faith factor* and transformed my life, my perception of Him and my comprehension of things spiritual.

I can tell you too that I am one of the many people who *has* been able to contact the Great Universal Spirit we call 'God', or, to be more precise, has been contacted *by* that Great Universal Spirit.

One thing of which *the faith factor* has convinced me is

that God is knowable to human beings, but only through a revelation to them *of* Himself made *by* Himself. God is beyond human understanding though not beyond human experience.

There is far more about God which I do *not* know than there is that I *do* know! Nevertheless, *the faith factor* has made such an astonishing difference to my perception of God that what I *do* know is well worth knowing and well worth telling!

The Apostle Paul was a man of outstanding intellect and an eminent theologian long before his conversion to Christianity yet, even after he had had the supernatural experience of seeing Jesus, he had to admit that his perception of God and of things spiritual was of necessity clouded, distorted and incomplete.

If he who met the resurrected and glorified Christ on the road to Damascus was not ashamed to admit that he saw the things of God 'through a glass darkly', then why should *anyone* be ashamed to admit that there are questions to which they do not have the answers, and things in the Divine revelation that they cannot understand completely or define precisely?

That should not discourage us though! One does not have to be an electrician to switch on the light nor is it necessary to understand the technicalities of transistors to be able to turn on the radio—it is sufficient to *have* a properly equipped receiver and to follow the instruction book. Only a small minority of those who regularly receive distinct transmissions through the marvels of modern technology—telephone, radio, television, satellite, etc—*really* understand the technicalities of how those things work, but they successfully receive the transmissions and that's all that matters.

I particularly like the old hymn in which the hymnwriter too confesses that there are so many things that *he does not know* but there is *one* thing that he does know beyond doubt. In the verses he catalogues the things he does not know but always returns in the chorus to 'But I *know whom I have believed* and am persuaded that He is able to keep that which I have committed unto him against that day.'

> I know not why God's wondrous grace
> To me He hath made known,
> Nor why, unworthy, Christ in love
> Redeemed me for His own—
>
> But I know whom I have believed,
> And am persuaded that He is able,
> To keep that which I've committed
> Unto Him against that day,
>
> I know not how this saving faith
> To me He did impart,
> Nor how believing in His Word
> Wrought peace within my heart—
>
> But I know whom I have believed,
> And am persuaded that He is able,
> To keep that which I've committed
> Unto Him against that day.
>
> I know not how the Spirit moves,
> Convincing men of sin,
> Revealing Jesus thro' the Word,
> Creating faith in Him—
>
> But I know whom I have believed,
> And am persuaded that He is able,
> To keep that which I've committed
> Unto Him against that day.

It was the Apostle Paul who wrote the words 'I know whom I have believed, and am persuaded that he is able to keep that which I have committed unto him against that day' (2 Timothy 1:12).

Paul too speaks of 'holding the *mystery* of the faith' (1 Timothy 3:9). He spoke of the rapture and the resurrection as being 'a mystery' (1 Corinthians 15:51) and of the wonderful peace which pervades the life of the believer as being 'the peace of God, *which passeth all understanding*' (Philippians 4:7).

Peter spoke of the unique joy that gushed forth from the innermost being of those who have received *the faith factor* as being 'joy *unspeakable* and full of glory' (1 Peter 1:8). There were times when these most eloquent of men could find no words to describe the *new dimension* of existence into which they had entered and the supernatural experiences which flooded their souls.

I freely admit to knowing nothing about God which God has not Himself revealed to me through *the faith factor*, through His Son Jesus Christ, through His Word the Bible and through His Holy Spirit!

Nobody can tell me that *the faith factor* does not exist, any more than they can tell a man who has just fallen off a ladder that the force of gravity does not exist! We have the best proof one can possibly have—we have experienced it for ourselves! I want to promise you, it is a promise born of personal experience, that, given the chance, *the faith factor* will *initiate you into a new dimension of existence and revolutionise your life*.

Some may wish I had dealt at more length and at greater depth with the doctrinal aspects of the Christian faith. I am more interested in showing my readers how to switch the receiver on and tune it in than initiating them into the art of taking the radio to pieces and showing them the technicalities of how it works. Anyway, as I have said, I don't really know how this receiver works, I only know that it *does* work.

I fully recognise that *all* Scripture is important (2 Timothy 3:16) but I have confined myself here to discussing only those things which relate directly to the reader's search for God. There are many things which I will avoid discussing in this book because my purpose is to direct the reader—I avoid the words 'lead the reader'—to Christ. To that end, with Paul, I have determined to know nothing among you save Jesus Christ and Him crucified (1 Corinthians 2:2).

Some will become irritated perhaps by my repetitious use and quotation of certain passages from the Bible. The reason I have repeated the same quotations often, and sometimes at length, is because I know that the readership for which I intend this book may well not be conversant with the passages and may be loath either to look back in this book to find the quotations or look them up in their Bibles. It is important that we proceed with the authority of the Bible emphasised at every point—so I keep certain scriptures before my reader continually.

Oh yes, how I wish I could ask you to follow me and in doing so assure you of salvation but, as I have said, I can't and no man can. I have not, nor has any other human being, any claim to goodness or rectitude of life which fits us for the task of leading men and women to Christ. At the most we can only plead a calling and an inner belief that this wonder we have experienced should be made known to others.

I have perhaps two qualifications for writing this book. The first is that I do not live in the religious environment as do some professional preachers and therefore I spend my working life among very much the same kind of person and in the same environment as the majority of my readers.

My second qualification is that I have found a *new dimension of existence* through *the faith factor* and *I have been where my reader now is* and *come from where my reader now is* to a knowledge of the one true and living God.

1 *'There must be more to life than this!'*

MILLIONS OF PEOPLE, many millions more than at any time in the history of our planet, are searching for the meaning of life in general and peace, tranquillity and contentment in their *own lives* in particular. That much can be discerned from the multitudes of people seeking and following a variety of strange religions and philosophies both ancient and modern.

It is not surprising that it should be so for we live, not only in the first generation with the ability to destroy our own planet and all the life upon it, but also in the first generation to have lost faith in the future.

Time was when we strove, quite rightly, for more sophistication and advancement in almost every sphere of human endeavour, believing that almost every affliction—political, national, social, family and individual—would succumb to the progress of human expertise.

It just has not happened like that! There is ample evidence to show that the nations with the highest standards of living and which have the most advanced technological skills have a higher incidence of suicide and drug abuse, a higher level of stress related mental illness, more violence on their streets and a higher incidence of the breakup of family life than less 'advanced' nations.

I was raised in what was then called a 'slum area'—we have nicer names for such places today—and folk had very little of this world's wealth but I never heard the words 'I'm bored' and 'I'm fed up' used with such frequency as I do now among people who believe themselves to have almost everything a person can desire.

We, as a society, have indeed come the full circle and lived to realise what Jesus meant when He said, 'Man does not live by bread alone'!

I am not 'downing' human progress when I say that— I merely make the point that material things have not succeeded in fulfilling the deeper, spiritual needs of man. As with so many wonderful medical drugs, human progress has its nasty side effects. Don't let's stop the progress, let's get rid of the nasty side effects!

Jesus did not tell us that man does not live by bread but that man does not live *by bread alone!* It is not only an inspired statement but also a shrewd observation even from a temporal point of view. Take away any of the important component parts from a piece of machinery and you will create malfunction. That man has a spiritual side to his nature is self-evident—to deny that spiritual side of humankind its essential expression is to invite malfunction.

There will, I know, be a wide consensus of agreement with me when I say that something has gone dreadfully wrong with our society, and that, because society is the sum total of the individual within it, something has gone dreadfully wrong with *people*.

As a businessman I know of no better way, when something has gone wrong with a product, than asking the maker to put it right!

Now when I write of a 'materialistic way of life' I do not mean a life in which material things are sought after and enjoyed—to achieve that is quite a proper ambition for anyone—but a way of life in which material things have taken the place of, or pre-eminence over, spiritual things.

There is a better way!

I am writing this book because I know from experience that *the faith factor* fulfils all that most people are seeking, but often failing to find, in today's materialistic way of life. I want to tell you about the way of life which brings perfect peace and contentment to those who will take a little time and trouble to study it and accept it.

Yes! I know that, for myself, I have found *a new dimension of life* and I hope to be able to convince you of it! I have within me a *freedom of spirit* which can only be explained by the words Jesus spoke when He said:

> If the Son shall make you free, ye shall be free indeed. John 8:36

There is a *peace* pervading my life which Paul the Apostle could only describe as:

> The peace of God, which passeth all understanding. Philippians 4:7

All my days I have been filled with such a *rapturous joy* that it is described in the Bible as being:

> Joy unspeakable and full of glory.   1 Peter 1:8

I have found an *unbounded contentment* in life which Paul spoke of when he said:

> I have learned in whatsoever state I am to be content.   Philippians 4:11

By experience I know what Jesus meant when He said:

> Whosoever drinketh of the water that I shall give him shall never thirst; but the water that I shall give him shall be in him a well of water springing up into everlasting life.   John 4:14

I am not one of great poetic ability or, I am sorry to say, appreciation—given, as I am, more to the appreciation of humorous doggerel than to anything of a more sensitive nature—but I *can* appreciate the truths expressed by the hymnwriter when he wrote:

> Loved with everlasting love,
> Led by grace that love to know,
> Spirit breathing from above,
> Thou hast taught me it is so,
> Oh, this full and perfect peace!
> Oh, this transport all divine!
> In a love which cannot cease,
> I am His and He is mine.
>
> Heaven above is softer blue,
> Earth around is sweeter green;
> Something lives in every hue
> Christless eyes have never seen,

> Birds with gladder songs o'erflow,
> Flowers with deeper beauties shine,
> Since I know as now I know,
> I am His and He is mine.
>
> Things that once were wild alarms
> Cannot now disturb my rest;
> Closed in everlasting arms,
> Pillowed on the loving breast:
> Oh, to lie for ever here!
> Doubt and care and self resign,
> While a whisper in my ear says—
> I am His and He is mine.
>
> His for ever, only His;
> Who my Lord and me shall part?
> Ah, with what a rest of bless,
> Christ can fill the longing heart!
> Heaven and earth may fade and flee;
> Firstborn light in gloom decline;
> But while God and I shall be,
> I am His and He is mine.

I have seen people under the influence of the drug LSD and seen how their perception of the world around them changes. That is, of course, why people take drugs—to change their perception of the world in which they live—to try and reach *a new dimension*.

There *is* a new dimension, as the hymnwriter so well expresses. It is every bit as revolutionary as the experience to be gained from any drug but, unlike the drug experience, it is permanent and *real*!

Something very unusual is happening to you!

The *natural* reaction of anyone coming across a book entitled *The Faith Factor* and proposing that there is a *new dimension* to life which relatively few people know about, is to smile, perhaps a little scornfully, and ignore it, for the Bible says:

> Natural man receiveth not the things of the Spirit of God; for they are foolishness unto him; *neither can he know them,* because they are spiritually discerned.   1 Corinthians 2:14

Inability to comprehend *the other dimension* is no new human malady nor my view of it a new theology. Charles Wesley wrote:

> Spirit of faith, come down,
> Reveal the things of God;
> And make to us the Godhead known,
> And witness with the blood.
>
> No man can truly say
> That Jesus Christ is Lord,
> Unless Thou take the veil away,
> And breathe the living word.

It is almost two thousand years since the Apostle Paul wrote:

> We speak the wisdom of God in a mystery, even *the hidden wisdom,* which God ordained before the ages unto our glory; which none of the princes of this age knew; for had they known it, they would

'THERE MUST BE MORE TO LIFE THAN THIS!'

not have crucified the Lord of glory.
1 Corinthians 2:7–8

Those are scriptures to which we will return time and time again in this book.

The very fact that you have decided to read this book, if you have decided to read this book, shows that something very unusual is taking place in your life—you have an interest in a subject in which, by nature, you would not have an interest. That is a sure and certain sign that God is seeking you, speaking to you, calling you and facing you with the greatest decision of your life.

Do you feel that 'there is more to life than this'?

God often speaks through circumstances—sometimes a vague feeling that there is more to life than the life one is living. At other times there may be a strange, disturbing feeling that one is not altogether fulfilling the purpose of one's existence. It's rather like thirst telling the body it needs liquid and we are not satisfied until we obtain something to drink. The feeling that there is something missing in life is a form of spiritual thirst which is *put there by God* to lead the enquirer to the one true fountain of life.

I remember having tea with a member of the English aristocracy—I will not mention his name for obvious reasons. It was a fine summer's evening and after tea we walked with his wife and children in the parkland of his palatial home. His estates stretched out to the woodlands which formed part of his land and beyond to a considerable lake which shimmered in the sunlight. I was just thinking that all this was some kind of heaven on earth when he said, 'You know there must be more to life than this'!

Of course there is! Beyond all our pride in our achievements, beyond all the pleasure and comfort we receive from our possessions, beyond all that the material world can offer there is a spiritual need in humankind which remains unsatisfied until a rapport exists with God.

If you are completely satisfied with life and feel no need of anything other than the material things and experiences you have, then I would ask you to consider whether you have really thought about life and its ultimate meaning. If, on the other hand, you have an area of dissatisfaction in your life, any area of dissatisfaction, then I would ask you to consider the possibility that the stirrings of dissatisfaction are nothing less than God moving you to seek Him.

'God,' the old hymn says, 'works in mysterious ways'!

There is nothing very significant about you having seen this book on the shelf of a bookshop, or having seen an advertisement for it in a newspaper, or having been given it by a friend but there is something very significant about your wanting to read it.

At first I had several 'trick titles' to hand—I haven't spent a considerable part of my life writing advertising copy to no purpose—they would undoubtedly have caused far more people to read the book but I discarded them knowing that the only way a person can come to know God is if God calls that person and reveals Himself to him.

Yes, I discarded the trick titles and decided to address the book to those who were searching for the One Great God of the Universe, knowing that it would then only reach a readership towards which God was already reaching out.

So I say, without any doubt in my mind whatsoever, that if you have the desire to read this book then *God is approaching you.* It only remains for you to listen to His voice and respond *so that you too can enter into this new dimension of life—a dimension you have hitherto not realised existed.*

2 *Why the 'you' in you will never die*

At the very heart of the teaching of Jesus Christ there are two vital propositions, the first being that each and every one of us survives death of the physical body.

The second proposition is that the power of God can transform our lives on this earth in the here-and-now. *The revolutionised life* can be the experience of each and every one of us. The Bible says:

> They that wait upon the Lord shall renew their strength; they shall mount up with wings as eagles; they shall run and not be weary; and they shall walk, and not faint.   Isaiah 40:31

In another passage the Bible says of Christ-centred life in the here-and-now:

> Thou [Jesus] will keep him in *perfect peace,* whose

mind is stayed on thee, because he trusteth in thee.
Isaiah 26:3

I have seen thousands of lives transformed by the power of God but that is something I will deal with later.

First I will deal with the first proposition of the gospel of Jesus Christ, that is, that *all* of us survive the death of the physical body. I will deal with it first for the simple, some will say simplistic, reason that eternity, the there-and-then, lasts a lot longer than the here-and-now.

Close-to-death experiences and after-death experiences

A programme appeared on television a few evenings ago; it was a transmission in the BBC Q.E.D. series and was entitled *Glimpses of Death*. The programme had nothing to do with religion, nothing to do with spiritualism and nothing to do with the occult; it had to do with scientific investigation.

Clinical Neurologist Dr Peter Fenwick of St Thomas's Hospital, London, who is collating evidence of near-death experiences and who appeared in the programme, is interested only in brain functions and the science of human consciousness.

Close-to-death experiences are not new. I think most people have been present when, or have heard of someone who was present when, a dying person 'saw something'. Perhaps the 'experience' was the recognition of a long dead loved one beckoning or of the Lord holding out His arms in welcome.

Comforting as such experiences are to those who accept them, statistics would seem to show that such 'visions' are a product of the human mind based upon what the person concerned would, conditioned by the environment in which they have lived, *expect* to see at the time of death. Evidence shows that those of a Christian culture tend to 'see' Jesus very much as He is depicted in religious art and 'heaven' as they imagine it is taught in the Christian gospel. People of other cultures tend to 'see' their own gods at the point of death and visions of the afterlife *their* religious training would lead them to expect.

Close-to-death experiences have, of course, always been known to doctors and they know that such experiences are usually medically explicable. Drugs can produce mystical experiences and so can anaesthetic.

Now we have a new kind of near-death experience— an *after*-death experience, an experience which was not possible even a few years ago. Hitherto all such experiences had been near-*this*-side-of-death experiences but what the programme I have mentioned concentrated on was near-the-*other*-side-of-death experiences.

Other-side-of-death experiences have not been encountered until now because only relatively recently has it been possible for doctors to actually bring people back from the dead. So we have this new phenomenon— the relating of after-death experiences by those who have been declared clinically dead but have been resuscitated!

So many after-death experiences have been reported by people who have been declared clinically dead that Dr Fenwick and other medical investigators into the nature of human consciousness are taking the investigation of the phenomenon seriously.

Medical investigators have now set out to explain the phenomenon within the confines of present medical knowledge. It is known, of course, that a person with a reduced oxygen supply to the brain, something which usually happens when a person is nearing death, may hallucinate and may well have some sort of mystical experience.

However, near-to-death experiences which are explicable by hallucination are of a very different order from the *after*-death experiences which were featured in this television programme!

Dr Michael B. Sabom, an American cardiologist, admits to having approached the subject with a great deal of scepticism, but later wrote a book, *Recollections of Death*, in which he recounts numerous accounts given to him by patients of after-death experiences. On the programme he told how doctors are now becoming deeply interested in the recollections of people who have been 'brought back' and have begun to gather into a body of scientific evidence such experiences. Both Dr Fenwick and Dr Sabom agreed that many of these experiences cannot be explained by anything that medical science knows about human consciousness.

A number of those who had died and been resuscitated told how, though they were clinically dead, they knew exactly what was going on around them. They had seen everything and heard everything that was happening to their body *after* death.

They *were* dead, needless to say unconscious, their eyes were closed, they were lying on their backs and, even had they been conscious, would have been able to see nothing but the ceiling of the hospital ward and the medics surrounding them. Yet, as I have said, they were able to tell the medics precisely what had been said and done during the time they were dead.

More surprisingly, they said that they had been looking down on their own bodies from a high vantage point—some said from the ceiling. They described accurately things which could only have been seen from a high vantage point because the people and equipment around them would have blocked their view from the bed upon which their bodies lay even had they been alive and well.

One told of seeing happenings in another room through a window though there was a screen between the bed and the window. What he said he saw was actually what happened in the next room during the time he was dead and could only have been seen by him if he had actually been viewing from ceiling height!

As Dr Fenwick pointed out, hallucinations brought on by drugs, anaesthetic or deprivation of oxygen would produce random experiences but the after-death experiences reported were surprisingly uniform.

It is no part of hallucination to be able to see actual events happening when one's eyes are closed! Dr Sabom thought of the possibility that his patients were recounting scenes that they had seen on television medical programmes but decided against that theory because what those who had come back from being clinically dead had reported were incidents that were *unique to their own treatment*.

Dr Sabom interviewed more people and then checked their hospital records to find that what they said they saw and heard happening to their bodies after they were dead was what actually *had* happened!

Both Dr Fenwick and Dr Sabom are rightly cautious in drawing scientific conclusions from their findings but it is evident from the work they have done so far that human consciousness exists *after* the death of the physical body.

Well done medical science! At least these two doctors

have faced up to a challenge it may well have been professionally more safe for them to have ignored. Some may think that it is a rather late stage for medical science to be investigating these things, but they could not have done so before because nobody who had been *really* dead had ever come back.

Now we are getting a glimpse of beyond the grave we are receiving also a glimpse of the *real* nature of humankind—that the human spirit, or soul, or consciousness survives the death of the human body.

Of course Jesus taught that almost two thousand years ago and, by faith, millions of people of all generations have known that human beings survive the death of the body in an aware and conscious form.

When the programme came to an end, I switched the television off and thought about it for several minutes. I wondered how the millions of people who died rejecting the teaching of Jesus about the afterlife and proclaiming 'When you're dead you're done for' felt those seconds after their death when they looked down on their dead body, realised they were still a conscious being and *knew* that they had been tragically wrong not to prepare for an eternal existence as Jesus had told them to!

Each of us has a spiritual 'mirror image'

Jesus has not only taught that we all survive the death of the physical body but that we *all* survive the death of the physical body in an identifiable and recognisable form. It would seem that the spiritual 'us' is nothing less than a mirror image of the physical 'us'.

He taught too that the condition and circumstances in which we live that eternal afterlife and the *quality* of our post-earthly existence is dependent upon our attitude to God in the person of Himself, Jesus Christ, in *this* life.

The Bible teaches that even the *physical body* is not for ever dispensed with at death, for further to teaching the survival of the non-body—the non-body being that which some call soul, others call spirit and some call by both names—there is the teaching of the resurrection of the *physical* body at some future time.

Jesus said:

> Marvel not at this; for the hour is coming, in the which all that are in the graves shall hear his voice, and shall come forth.   John 5:28

Such importance did Jesus give to the fact that the human spirit survives death in a fully conscious and aware form that He said:

> Fear not them who kill the body, but are not able to kill the soul; but rather fear him who is able to destroy both soul and body in hell. Matthew 10:28

There's a very real danger to a very real part of you!

Have you ever felt that there is a *you* which exists within and separately from the body? If so you are right! When Jesus spoke about the soul He spoke about the *real* you, the you which *inhabits* your physical body, not a you that depends upon your physical body for its existence.

The 'after-death' world

We see that Jesus spoke of 'hell' but He also spoke of another 'after-death' form of existence when He said:

WHY THE 'YOU' IN YOU WILL NEVER DIE

> Let not your heart be troubled; ye believe in God, believe also in me. In my Father's house are many mansions; if it were not so, I would have told you. I go to prepare a place for you. And if I go and prepare a place for you, I will come again, and receive you unto myself, that where I am, there ye may be also.　　　　　　　　　　John 14:1–3

The Bible makes it plain that the believer survives the death of the body and enters, *immediately* upon the death of the physical body, into the presence of Jesus. The Apostle Paul writes:

> We are confident, I say, and willing rather to be absent from the body, and to be present with the Lord.　　　　　　　　　　2 Corinthians 5:8

We find the same truth emphasised by Jesus at the crucifixion. Two thieves were crucified with Him. One of them turned to Jesus in his dying moments and said:

> Lord, remember me when thou comest into thy kingdom.

Jesus replied:

> Verily I say unto thee, *today* thou shalt be with me in paradise.　　　　　　　　　　Luke 23:42,43

Two forms of after-death existence

Jesus taught that there are *two* forms of existence after the death of the body and that *now* is the time to prepare for whichever form of after-death existence you wish to experience.

Some theologians may debate the meaning of the word 'hell' in my quotation from Matthew 10:28 but there are things in the meaning of it which are beyond dispute by any reasonable person.

The first thing is that it is better to suffer the death of the body at the hands of a cruel persecutor than to risk the 'destruction' of the soul. This indicates that, however one wishes to interpret the word 'hell', the condition in which a person who has died outside of the saving grace of Jesus Christ finds himself or herself *after* the death of the physical body, is horrific indeed. It is a thing terrible beyond description to die outside of the saving grace of Jesus Christ.

It would be so easy at this point to drift into a discussion about the nature of the place and condition which Jesus calls 'hell'. Sufficient though to say that one does not have to know the technicalities of a nuclear weapon to appreciate that it is better not to be there when it goes off!

When we are told by the highest authority in the universe 'Fear not them who kill the body, but are not able to kill the soul; but rather fear him who is able to destroy both soul and body in hell', then the precise nature of the place Jesus called 'hell' becomes something of an irrelevance, not to the theologian perhaps, but to those who at this moment wish to plan their eternal destiny.

If one is threatened by a great danger in any sphere of life then the sensible thing to do is to escape the danger first and leave the finer details for later discussion.

There *are* some things certain though.

Hell is not what we make this life

In the Matthew 10:28 statement of Jesus there is inherent an absolute refutation of the rather thoughtless idea that 'Hell is what we make this life.' If hell is what we make this life then obviously the destruction of the body under any circumstance would bring about the *end* of the state of 'hell'. Jesus makes it quite plain that the state which He warns us to avoid is something that exists, not in this life, but in the life *after* the death of the physical body.

We are told in the Bible that:

> It is appointed unto men *once* to die, but *after* this the judgment. Hebrews 9:27

Jesus drew aside the veil of death for a few moments when He told the story of two men who had entered upon different forms of post-death existence:

> There was a certain rich man, who was clothed in purple and fine linen, and fared sumptuously every day.
>
> And there was a certain beggar, named Lazarus, who was laid at his gate, full of sores.
>
> And desired to be fed with crumbs which fell from the rich man's table; moreover, the dogs came and licked his sores.
>
> And it came to pass that the beggar died, and was carried by the angels into Abraham's bosom; the rich man also died and was buried;
>
> And in hell he lifted up his eyes, being in torments, and seeth Abraham afar off, and Lazarus in his bosom.
>
> And he cried and said, Father Abraham, have mercy on me, and send Lazarus, that he may dip

the tip of his finger in water, and cool my tongue; for I am tormented in this flame.

But Abraham said, Son, remember that thou in thy lifetime receivedst thy good things, and likewise Lazarus evil things; but now he is comforted, and thou art tormented.

And beside all this, between us and you there is a great gulf fixed, so that they who would pass from here to you cannot; neither can they pass to us, that would come from there.

Then he said, I pray thee therefore, father, that thou wouldst send him to my father's house (For I have five brethren), that he may testify unto them, lest they also should come into this place of torment.

Abraham saith unto him, If they hear not Moses and the prophets, neither will they be persuaded, though one rose from the dead.   Luke 16:19–31

Some have contended that the story of a rich man and Lazarus is no more than a parable and, though it is not in the form of any other of the parables, I do not intend to take issue with them—I simply do not know and neither do they.

Be that as it may, we have to realise that a parable is spoken to elucidate and not confuse. There is no parable of Jesus which is not based upon fact. There is, for example, no incident in the parable of the prodigal son which could *not* happen. There is no incident in any other parable which was not a fact of life.

By definition a parable is an earthly story with a spiritual meaning, something with which we are familiar which is likened to and illustrative of something with which we are not familiar. If the narrative of the rich man and Lazarus is simply a parable then it is the only time Jesus reversed the role of the parable and took something with which his hearers were not familiar to illustrate—to illustrate what?

Accepting that the narrative of the rich man and Lazarus is a parable and parable is a method by which Jesus used things with which we are familiar to illustrate things with which we are not familiar—what then do we learn from the story of the rich man and Lazarus?

Firstly, that *all* human beings survive the death of the mortal body in a conscious and recognisable form.

Secondly, that our responses in this life denominate how we will spend that life beyond the death of the body.

Thirdly, that the human spirit, or the soul, is, after the death of the body, capable of enjoying pleasurable or tormenting experiences just as is the human body prior to death of the body.

Fourthly, that there will come a time when those who are existing in what Jesus calls 'hell' will wish they had done something about their own eternal salvation and the eternal salvation of those who are dear to them—but it will be too late.

Whether or not the rich man and Lazarus were actual people and whether or not the incidents said to have taken place during the lifetimes of the two were actual incidents that took place with the two men as participants is not important. There still remains the fact that, even as a parable, the story must mean *something*. If we do not accept the above four points then the story has no meaning whatsoever.

We must read the story of the rich man and Lazarus too in the context of the other statements of Jesus about 'hell'.

If human justice demands that there shall be no

punishment until after trial and after judgement then, as the justice of God is no less, who could say of a just God that He would punish *before* judging? Besides, who could support the proposition that it is always the most sinful people upon whom circumstances inflict the most 'hellish' lives?

That the place Jesus called 'hell' exists beyond the grave is reinforced by Jesus in the narrative of the rich man and Lazarus. As we have seen, Lazarus was a poor man who suffered privation in this life and the rich man we are told 'fared sumptuously every day'. If we are to accept the theory that hell is what we make this life then obviously the rich man had a life of 'heaven on earth' and the poor man had a life of 'hell on earth', but that is not what Jesus tells us.

What frightened Jesus?

Not long before He was crucified Jesus, facing death on the cross, prayed in the Garden of Gethsemane which is at the foot of the Mount of Olives. This is what the Bible says about His agony in the garden.

> And he came out, and went, as he was accustomed, to the Mount of Olives; and his disciples also followed him.
>
> And when he was at the place, he said unto them, Pray that ye enter not into temptation.
>
> And he was withdrawn from them about a stone's throw and kneeled down, and prayed,
>
> Saying, Father, if thou be willing, remove this cup from me; nevertheless, not my will, but thine, be done.

And there appeared an angel unto him from heaven, strengthening him.

And being in agony, he prayed more earnestly; and his sweat was, as it were, *great drops of blood falling down to the ground.* Luke 22:39–44

For many years people doubted the accuracy of that biblical record—few had witnessed someone sweating 'as it were' great drops of blood. Now we know it to be something that happens when a person is in great fear.

Why was Jesus in such great fear? He was to be crucified and He knew it, but thousands of people faced crucifixion in those days without displaying such fear. Think of the fortitude of the millions who have died in war! Think of Japanese pilots who during the war took off knowing that they were to crash their planes into enemy ships and die, often in an inferno! Think of today's terrorists who commit themselves to the most horrible deaths without flinching! Think of the many Christian martyrs who, though burned alive, did not display the fear that Jesus showed.

Then why did Jesus have such a fear that He sweated, as it were, great drops of blood?

Peter writing of Jesus says, 'Who his own self bore our sins in his own body on the tree [cross]' (1 Pet 2:24).

When Jesus died, perfect though He was, He died the death of a sinner bearing the sins of the world in His own body. That's why Jesus cried on the cross 'My God, my God, why hast thou forsaken me?'—He who was without sin was dying the death of a sinner. God always turns from sin.

Jesus sweated great drops of blood because *He knew what lay the other side of death*—He is the only man ever to die who *did* know fully what lay the other side of death for one who has not received *the faith factor*.

Jesus said:

> If thy hand offend thee, cut it off; it is better for thee to enter life maimed than, having two hands, to go into hell. Mark 9:43

Someone once said to me, 'I am not afraid of being dead but I *am* afraid of the process of dying.' They were wrong! Jesus taught that, unless we are prepared for death, being dead is far worse than the process of dying, however agonising that process may be. Jesus did not fear the agonising pain of death on the cross but He *did* fear passing beyond the grave with the sins of the world on His shoulders and facing that place and condition He called 'hell'.

People can indeed die bravely if they believe that death is the grand anaesthetic which brings oblivion or are not fully aware of what faces them the other side of the grave. Sentiment is a poor counsellor in view of the clear statements of Jesus about what lies beyond the grave.

The here-and-now decision

The inescapable conclusion to be drawn from the teaching of Jesus must be that *beyond* the physical death of the mortal body there is an existence that can be *ecstatically delightful* if we die in one set of circumstances but *indescribably horrific* if we die in another set of circumstances. *The only man to die who knew what lay beyond the grave for the unsaved soul, sweated as it were great drops of blood in terror at what faced Him—what He saw was so horrific!*

A tailor-made eternity?

The majority of people have some instinct, if not belief, that human beings survive the death of the body. Unfortunately they also seem to think that the life after death can be tailor-made to suit them. Rather than fitting themselves to eternity they attempt to fit eternity to themselves and create their own illusion of life after death.

You cannot change the nature of the after-death state by wishful thinking or by groundless imagination about what it is like. The after-death state is what it is; no amount of wishful thinking will alter the facts. One day we all have to face it, not the way you or I would *like* it to be but *the way it is and always has been.*

Those places to which human spirits pass at death are beyond human wit to manipulate or vary. The only control we have is to decide *which* of the choices open to us we will make.

As I have said, it is not our purpose to conduct a theological discussion on the nature of the spiritual places and conditions Jesus called 'heaven' and 'hell'. I have heard some very dogmatic expositions on the subject which have gone far beyond anything we read in the Bible. It is sufficient to stand firmly on the statements of Jesus and affirm that losing one's life or losing one's limbs is of far less importance than losing one's soul in 'hell'.

Jesus put life and afterlife into perspective when he said:

> For what is a man profited if he shall gain the whole world and lose his own soul? Matthew 16:26

If that means anything then surely it means that everything this world can offer becomes insignificant in the light of eternity.

The choice is ours—now!

What Jesus came to tell us was that we can determine *how* and *where* we shall spend eternity—now!

There is a way in which we can make sure of our eternal destiny *without any doubt whatsoever*.

Jesus said:

> He that heareth my word, and believeth in him that sent me, *hath [has got]* everlasting life, and shall not come into condemnation; but *is* passed from death unto life. John 5:24

Notice the present tense words in that statement. 'Hath'—it means that if you fulfil the conditions you start your everlasting life *now*, not when you die; there is an instant improvement in not only the length but also the quality of your existence. *Eternal life* is not only a different quantity of life in the there-and-then but a different quality of life in the here-and-now—*a new dimension*. You have the promise of Jesus that you will 'never come into condemnation' but that you will, at the very moment you fulfil the conditions He imposes, pass from death unto life. I will return to that promise laterr.

The resurrection of the body

We have seen that the non-body, the soul or spirit, survives the death of the body. The teaching of Jesus goes much further than that though and affirms that the physical body is raised again from the dead at some future time.

The Bible says:

> Marvel not at this; for the hour is coming, in the which *all* that are in the graves shall hear his voice, and shall come forth: they that have done good, unto the resurrection of life; and they that have done evil, unto the resurrection of damnation.
>
> John 5:28–29

That that refers to the physical body is self-evident since it is by definition impossible for a spirit to be in the grave.

The Bible expands this concept of the resurrection of the *mortal body* when Paul writes to those who believe in Christ:

> Behold I show you a mystery: we shall not all sleep, but we shall all be changed, in the moment, in the twinkling of an eye, at the last trump; for the trumpet shall sound, *and the dead shall be raised incorruptible,* and we shall be changed. For this corruptible must put on incorruption, and this mortal must put on immortality. So, when this corruptible shall have put on incorruption, and this mortal shall have put on immortality, then shall be brought to pass the saying that is written, Death is swallowed up in victory.

> O death, where is thy sting? O grave, where is thy victory?
>
> 1 Corinthians 15:51–55

The importance of knowing about the future life

We humans have, quite rightly, expended considerable time, effort, money and energy improving the *quality* of life *on this earth* and that is altogether right and proper. What is altogether wrong is that many people give very little consideration to the beyond-the-grave existence.

Jesus *never* condemned success, indeed many Bible precepts go a long way to ensuring success. I think that whatever success I have had in life has come about when I have obeyed the precepts of Jesus and whatever failures I have had have come about when I have not obeyed the precepts of Jesus.

The exhortation to 'Be not slothful in business' (Romans 12:11) is a sure recipe for success in business and 'Whatever thy hand findeth to do, do it with all thy might' (Ecclesiastes 9:10) is a recipe for success in any walk of life. The warning of Jesus is not against gaining the whole world but against losing one's soul in the process.

I personally have always been ambitious and I must admit to enjoying in full my life on this earth. I am an enthusiast for living. I am an enthusiastic supporter of any progress which makes this earth a better place to live and of any legitimate means by which an individual can improve his lot here.

Is it not irrational, though, that most people have not a similar dedication to ensuring their quality of life in the world to come? Is it not a bit unbalanced, I use the word advisedly, to devote oneself entirely to the short here-and-now when there is such a long there-and-then to face when we have left our physical bodies, temporarily, behind?

The central theme of the Bible is that there is a vital choice to be made and that *you* should not hesitate to make it now.

3 *You have a problem!*

YOU HAVE A PROBLEM—there's a part of you missing!

Despite what *you* may think it's the most vital part of you too!

The strange thing is that people don't even notice that it *is* missing—*you* may not have noticed this part of *you* to be missing.

Do *you* have difficulty in *really* believing? Do you *really believe* that Jesus was God manifest in the flesh? Do you *really believe* that Jesus was born of a virgin? Do you *really believe* that Jesus was quite literally and physically raised from the dead? Do you *really believe* that the Bible is the inspired word of God?

I emphasise *really believe* because there is a difference between just 'going along with' what one has always been taught and is expected to believe and *really believing*.

If you have difficulty in *really believing*—don't worry

YOU HAVE A PROBLEM! 47

about it! You are perfectly normal or, as the Bible puts it, 'natural'. *You* are not to be blamed for not comprehending these things any more than your vacuum cleaner is to be blamed for not picking up radio signals—it's not equipped to pick up radio signals and *you* are not at present equipped to comprehend the spiritual world.

The Apostle Paul wrote:

> We speak, not in the words which man's wisdom teacheth, but which the Holy Spirit teacheth, comparing spiritual things with spiritual. *But the natural man receiveth not the things of the Spirit of God;* for they are foolishness to him, neither can he know them, because they are *spiritually* discerned.
> 1 Corinthians 2:13–14

You won't necessarily receive a transmission because you read an instruction book

Let me illustrate by taking the example of a television set.

Perhaps you are old enough to remember the days when there was only one television channel. When other channels came on the air viewers either had to purchase new sets or have new parts fitted to their existing sets to enable them to receive the new transmission. *Until that missing part was fitted no amount of reading the instruction book would enable the viewer to cause the set to pick up the new channel.*

The owner of the old type set could have been forgiven for assuming that no other channel than the *one* channel was transmitting because, whatever he did, however thoroughly he followed the instruction book and however many knobs he twiddled, the new vision would not appear.

Similarly *you* may have listened to a lot of instructions (sermons) and read the Bible (the instruction book) but without establishing communication with God. You may have *really* tried to make contact but such contact has eluded you. As with the television set which could not receive a new transmission until it had received the missing part so *you* will not be able to receive a knowledge of spiritual things until *you* have received *your* 'missing part'.

I am writing these words on the word processing program of a computer. I have been working this computer now for three years and yet it is only a few days ago that a representative of the computer company showed me a program stored in the memory of the computer which I hadn't got the slightest idea was there. There was no way in which I could bring it to the screen until I knew the 'password'. I asked that computer expert what would have been the chance of me opening that program 'by accident'. He said the odds against me doing that were so enormous as to be not worth considering.

However much you read, however much you are told, you will not succeed in contacting God until you have the password and the 'missing part' planted by God Himself within you.

You see, finding God is not an intellectual search—it is a *esoteric happening!*

When colour transmissions began, owners of black-and-white sets faced a similar problem as their one-channel predecessors had—they could not receive transmissions in colour. They saw everything in black and white though that was not the way it was being transmitted. *Which illustrates the fact that things are not always the way you perceive them!*

Unless the owners of black-and-white sets had heard about colour transmissions, read about them or believed those who already had, or had seen, colour sets, they would not have known colour transmission was happening.

The fact is that without the 'new part' you can no more know God than you receive colour pictures on a black-and-white television set.

A blank screen does not mean that there is no transmission taking place!

Staying for a moment with the modern parable of the television set, if during transmission hours tonight your television went blank and you tried all the channels only to find that the screen remained blank, you would not assume that the transmission had ceased, would you? Your response would be to assume that something had gone wrong with *your* receiver and it was therefore not picking up the transmissions.

Perhaps you have assumed, because you have never had an experience with God, that He does not exist or that to know God is beyond the ken of humankind; but is that a valid assumption? Will you consider for one moment another possibility—*that your receiver is defective?* That God does not exist or is unknowable is not a reasoned or reasonable conclusion to draw from the fact that *you* have never had an experience with God.

Stop for a moment and consider the millions of people all over the world who say they *have* made contact with and had an experience of God!

A few such people may well be, of course, simple,

superstitious people but millions of them are anything but simple and anything but superstitious. The fact is that there is no strata of society, no social class, no nationality, no age group, no profession, no Intelligence Quotient and no income level which does not contain people who claim to have made contact with God. Most such people have nothing to gain and everything to lose in the natural world if they are *pretending* to know God. Why should such people lay themselves open to ridicule and harassment for that which they know to be untrue?

Throughout the centuries many have been put to death for their faith and, even today, death and imprisonment is, in many more countries than it should be, the lot of those who tell of having an experience with God.

Even admitting that it is possible that some people may have suffered a form of delusion, I cannot think that the *millions* of people, in every generation since the world began who have testified to a similar experience, are the victims of delusion. Will you consider for a moment that the problem *may* be with your reception system?

Of course I respect your right to doubt whether God exists, after all you cannot help doubting if you really do doubt, but I think that you would be unwise to ignore the possibility that your lack of awareness of God has more to do with your inability to receive His transmissions than it has to do with His non-existence.

So contemplate for a moment the millions of people all over the world, of every race, of every level of education, rich and poor, who have said that they have experienced communication with God and ask yourself why they *have* and you *have not*. Why should they say it if it were not true?

Is there a sixth sense?

Would you dare to say, would it be a valid assumption, that all these people are misguided, unbalanced or untruthful? And remember, it does not take a large number of people to have had an experience with God to prove it possible—if just one of all those many millions of people is right then it proves the possibility of communication with God. To deny the existence of God, to deny the possibility of humankind communicating with God *you have to say that each and every one of those millions of people are dishonest or mistaken!*

The alternative is to consider the possibility that, as with the television set, they have a part, a receptor, in them that you have not got; a receptor which enables them to pick up a communication that you have not had. You have five senses—is it possible that there is a *sixth* sense which humankind once had but which at some time, for some reason, it lost? it's worth finding out isn't it?

For me to say to you 'All you have to do is to accept what I am saying' is rather like me saying to a blind person 'All you have to do is see.' In fact the Bible often likens the inability to 'see' spiritually to the inability to see physically.

Remember that blindness is the *inability* to see, not a desire *not* to see!

Jesus spotlighted this inability to 'see' spiritually when, quoting Isaiah. He said:

> He hath blinded their eyes, and hardened their heart; that they should not see with their eyes, nor understand.   John 12:40

Here's the 'part name' of the new part you need to receive the spiritual transmission

The part name is *'faith'* but I don't want you to stop reading because I do not mean by 'faith' what some people mean by faith. I do not mean 'blind belief'—so many people have a mistaken idea of what faith is, what faith does and how it is to be obtained.

The faith factor is to knowing God what the microscope is to knowing about microbes!

The faith factor is to knowing about God what the telescope is to knowing about astronomy!

The faith factor is to knowing about God what a tuned television set is to the television transmission.

The faith factor opens up otherwise unseen worlds, elevates us to a *new dimension* of consciousness and brings about new experiences that you may have heard talked about, sometimes doubted and never experienced.

The Bible says:

> For by grace are ye saved, through *faith;* and that *not of yourselves: it is the gift of God:* not of works, lest any man should boast. Ephesians 2:8

I'll deal with the word 'grace' later; sufficient now to say that it means 'unmerited favour'.

The Bible says:

> Faith is the *substance* of things hoped for, the *evidence* of things not seen. Hebrews 11:1

You have often said, 'If only I could see God, speak with God, touch God I would believe.' You find it difficult to comprehend a spirit and you can't be blamed for that!

What you mean is that you want substance—*the faith factor* gives you substance!

You want evidence—*the faith factor* gives you evidence!

I promise you that once you have received this missing part you will find it just as impossible not to believe as you do now to believe.

Here's something very important that you should remember. Write it down on a piece of paper and keep it before you:

> FAITH IS NOT BELIEVING—FAITH IS THE
> GOD-IMPARTED ABILITY TO BELIEVE.

Faith is equivalent to the part you put into that old channel one set which makes it capable of receiving other transmissions. Faith is the eye with which you see God. Faith is the ear with which you hear the voice of God. Faith is the hand with which you touch God! *Faith can be obtained in no other way than by asking God for it and receiving it as a free gift from God.*

4 *The faith factor*

Now we all know what a gift is. It's not something you work for, it's not necessarily something you deserve, it's something you get because someone wants to give it to you. A gift is not something you generate within yourself or purchase for yourself, it is something that comes to you free and without charge from outside.

Another thing that it is important to realise about a gift is that though anyone can *buy a gift for you* no one can *give you a gift* unless you are prepared to receive it.

All that applies to the gift of faith—*the faith factor*.

You have to use the correct tool for any job!

You do not write a letter with a screwdriver nor drive a screw with a pen—there is a correct tool for every job. Use the wrong tool and you will soon become convinced that the job can't be done.

If you have become convinced that you cannot communicate with God then ask yourself if you have been using the correct 'tool' for the job.

There have been many billions of microbes in existence since the earth began but our grandfathers did not know they were there.

Billions of stars have thronged the heavens since time began but our forebears were able to see but a few of them—they had not got the means to see them.

Then someone discovered the microscope and suddenly that which had existed all the time became discernible by human eyes. The microbes had been there but the means by which they could be seen had not been there. The scientist had *discovered a new part*—the microscope.

Someone invented the telescope and, later, more powerful telescopes, and stars came into view which the eye of man had hitherto been unable to comprehend. The astronomer had *discovered a new part* which enabled him to see things he had never been able to see before.

What I am saying is that *Christianity is a revealed religion.* And the 'tool' through which you comprehend that which is otherwise obscured from you is *the faith factor.*

> For the preaching of the cross is to them that perish foolishness; but unto us who are saved it is the power of God.
>
> For it is written, I will destroy the wisdom of the wise, and will bring to nothing the understanding of the prudent.
>
> Where is the wise? Where is the scribe? Where is the disputer of this age? Hath not God made foolish the wisdom of this world?

> For after that, in the wisdom of God, the world by wisdom knew not God, it pleased God by the foolishness of preaching to save them that believe.
> 1 Corinthians 1:18–21

Knowledge of God is not something you can perceive by study or learning, though study and learning can subsequently help. A study of the sky at night would lead you to believe many erroneous things if you didn't study it through a telescope, and to look at a sheet of glass would lead you to believe, if you believed the evidence of your eyes, that there was no life on that piece of glass when in fact it was teeming with life.

Contemplate for a moment what would happen if you tried to study microbes through the finest telescope in the world or stars through the finest microscope obtainable. Your resulting knowledge would be far less than if you had studied them with the naked eye!

Just as a screwdriver is not the correct instrument with which to write a letter, the pen is not the correct instrument with which to drive a screw, the telescope is *not* the correct instrument through which one should study microbes and the microscope is not the correct instrument with which to study the stars so any other 'instrument' than *faith* is the wrong instrument to 'see' God.

There's an invisible world all around us

Time was when it seemed rational to say 'I only believe in that which I see', but not in this modern age. We now know that there are more things in existence which *do not* respond to the unaided human senses than things that do.

I have mentioned stars and microbes but as I write

there are singers singing and orchestras playing in my study but I can't hear them. Radio waves cannot be heard by the unaided human ear and television pictures cannot be seen by the unaided human eye—we need a properly tuned radio or television set. *Things which do not respond to the unaided human senses are all around us in profusion—God is just one of those things.*

How to obtain the missing part

We have seen that *the faith factor* is the *gift* of God and you will understand from that, that the only way for you to get it is for *you* to ask for it, *God* to give it to you and for *you* to be willing to receive it.

The faith factor is not something you can generate within yourself *however hard you may try*.

Jesus said:

> Ask, and it shall be given you; seek, and ye shall find; knock, and it shall be opened unto you. For *everyone* that asketh receiveth; and he that seeketh findeth; and to him that knocketh it shall be opened. Luke 11:9–10

'Ask', 'seek', 'knock'—three different things you have to do to get to know God.

You have to *ask* for the right thing in the correct way, you have to *seek* in the right place for the correct experience and you have to *knock* on the correct door.

Though no effort of yours can contribute to your salvation there has to be determination on your part to 'ask', 'seek' and 'knock'. 'God,' says the Bible, 'is a rewarder of them that diligently seek him' (Hebrews 11:6).

You do not give precious gifts to insincere people do you? How would you react if you had bought a very expensive gift for someone and when you asked them to collect it they made no effort to do so?

How can anyone reasonable expect the God of the universe to grant a revelation of Himself to someone who will make no effort to ask, seek and knock?

God deals with each person as an individual

I think it to be a pity when anyone thinks of himself or herself as being 'one of the crowd'. God does not think of you in that way—He thinks of you as an individual! God deals with people in different ways and I don't know precisely how He will deal with you. The one thing I *do* know is that if you sincerely ask then He will answer and He will answer in an unmistakable way. I know too that salvation is always instantaneous—when you ask Jesus Christ to save you He does so at that moment!

I have mentioned the thief who died with Jesus and how he instantaneously secured his quality of life in the hereafter when he cried, 'Lord remember me when thou comest into thy kingdom', and Jesus replied, 'Verily I say unto you, today thou shalt be with me in paradise.' I don't know how long God had been working on that thief before He brought him to that place of acceptance, maybe years or maybe for a few seconds, but I do know that *immediately* that thief called upon the name of the Lord he was *instantaneously* saved!

In Acts 9 we read that Saul of Tarsus, who later became known as the Apostle Paul, had a rather different experience. It would seem that God strove with him for some time before he finally submitted himself to the divine revelation.

Why a criminal recognised what religious leaders missed

Read the Bible account carefully and try to 'see' that crucifixion scene. I am sure the priests, had they known Jesus to be God, would not have had Him crucified and the crowd, had *they* known Jesus to be God, would not have had Him crucified.

Consider for a moment the participants in the events of that fateful crucifixion day. There were the priests, men trained to expect and proclaim the coming of the Messiah, men who were conversant with the Scriptures which foretold when, where and how the Messiah would be born. They were actually living through the events foretold in their Scriptures, Scriptures they had doubtless read to their congregations on many occasions. These were theologians, men of intellect and groomed to a high standard of learning yet they did not recognise the person hanging on the cross.

I don't think that looking at the thing from a natural point of view we can blame them, for Jesus of Nazareth at this point in His life had done little that the neutral mind would associate with one who was to be the great deliverer. He had turned water into wine but then Moses had parted the Red Sea and Moses wasn't the Messiah! Jesus had healed the afflicted but Joshua had caused the walls of Jericho to fall and Joshua wasn't the Messiah! Jesus had walked upon the water but Elijah had been caught up into heaven in a chariot of fire and Elijah wasn't the Messiah! Jesus had not called fire down from heaven in any Sodom and Gomorrah-type episode nor brought waters to flood the earth as in the days of Noah, nor caused the sun to stand still as in the days of Joshua. Jesus had been whipped, humiliated, spat upon and now

He was dying—looking not at all like a God, a king or a messiah.

No human learning and no human knowledge could deduce from the sight of Jesus hanging on the cross other than that He was an ordinary man. There *were* people in the crowd though who knew who Jesus was! While *many* Roman soldiers cast lots for Jesus' clothes, *one* Roman soldier recognised who Jesus was and exclaimed, 'Truly this was the Son of God.' What 'inside knowledge' did that Roman soldier, who had probably not seen any of the prophecies of the coming Messiah, have which the other Roman soldiers and the Jewish holy men had not got! If Jesus had heard that Roman soldier He would no doubt have said to him, as He had said to Peter, 'Blessed art thou... for flesh and blood hath not revealed it to you but my Father which is in heaven.' *That soldier had received the faith factor* and consequently the crucifixion scene meant something very different to him from what it meant to those who jeered and mocked! It was not a difference in fact but a difference in perception.

No, Jesus didn't look at all like a god, or a king for that matter, as He hung there on the cross bloody, beaten, exhausted and mocked. Why did the dying thief recognise something in Jesus at that moment which the priests did *not* recognise? How could a man with little education and presumably no theological training recognise something which the theologians of the day did not comprehend? The answer is that the thief had *the faith factor*. He was given a spiritual perception that bypassed mere religious tradition, leapt over credibility fences, cut through the obvious and saw in the battered figure of the dying man next to him—*the Lord of Glory*. The other thief saw Jesus through *natural eyes* and therefore did not see in Him *the Lord of Glory*.

Two different groups of people divided on this issue, not by behaviour patterns, nationality or religion, survey the scene, hear the same utterances and mix with the same crowd but come to different conclusions about what they are witnessing. The difference is in their perception of the event. One group see a figure of fun being crucified and the other *the Lord of Glory*.

The roll of faith

There is in the Bible a whole chapter devoted to the subject of *faith*. I think I can do no better than to quote at length from it:

> Now faith is the substance of things hoped for, the evidence of things not seen.
>
> For by it the elders received witness.
>
> Through faith we understand that the worlds were framed by the word of God, so that things which are seen were not made of the things which do appear.
>
> By faith Abel offered unto God a more excellent sacrifice than Cain, by which he obtained witness that he was righteous, God testifying of his gifts; and by it he being dead yet speaketh. [See Genesis 4:2–7.]
>
> By faith Enoch was translated that he should not see death, and was not found, because God had translated him; for before his translation he had his testimony, that he pleased God.
>
> But without faith it is impossible to please him; for he that cometh to God must believe that he is, and that he is a rewarder of them that *diligently seek* him. [See Genesis 5:22–24.]

> By faith Noah, being warned of God of things not seen as yet, moved with fear, prepared an ark to the saving of his house, by which he condemned the world, and became heir of the righteousness which is by faith. [See Genesis chapters 6, 7 and 8.]
>
> By faith Abraham, when he was called to go out into a place which he should after receive for an inheritance, obeyed; and he went out, not knowing where he went. [See Genesis 12:1–4]
>
> By faith he sojourned in the land of promise, as in a foreign country, dwelling in tents with Isaac and Jacob, the heirs with him of the same promise; For he looked for a city which hath foundations whose builder and maker is God. Hebrews 11:1–10

So the roll of faith goes on and I would suggest the reader turn to it in the Bible and read through to the end.

It will be seen from those incidents of faith in action that one cannot take the produce of faith and tie it in neat little bundles or contain it within the confines of specific baskets. The *faith factor* is nothing more or less than, yes I will repeat it again, *the God-given ability to get into contact with God.*

The one prime lesson we learn from 'The Roll of Faith' is that 'By faith' each of the people mentioned came to know about the one true God and His purpose for them in their lives. By faith they not only knew about God but also obeyed His revealed will for them.

By faith Abel was brought to a recognition of the *acceptable sacrifice for sin.*

By faith Abraham *set out on an earthly pilgrimage.*

By faith Noah *was able to recognise a danger* and save himself and his family.

THE FAITH FACTOR

By faith Moses was able *to recognise he was in the wrong family and join God's people.*

Though so diverse the experiences of these people, they had this one thing in common—they all recognised something which was not obvious or even discernible by human research or human knowledge.

The way that seemeth right...

The Bible says:

> There is *a way which seemeth right* unto a man,
> but the end thereof are the ways of death.
> Proverbs 14:12

Most people do not set out to do wrong—they sincerely believe that they are doing right! Tell them that they are doing wrong and they will laugh you to scorn or, if they are very charitable folk, simply ignore you. *There is a way that seemeth right unto man!*

I think that most people, in the natural way of thought, would agree with Cain and worship God by bringing gifts of whatever the work of their hands produced! Does it not seem right that a person should thank God for the skills he has been given by returning to God the fruits of those gifts? Ah yes! That is what *natural man* thinks but God says, 'And almost all things are by the law purged with blood; and without shedding of blood is no remission' (Hebrews 9:22). There is no way that either Cain or Abel could have known that though because it had not at that time been revealed. How did Abel 'know' the right thing to do to please God? The Bible says, 'By *faith* Abel offered to God a more excellent sacrifice than Cain.' The contrast is between Cain who hoped to *reason* his way into God's favour and Abel who accepted *revealed religion*.

Abel did not follow *the way that seemeth right unto man!*

There is no human way Abraham could have known that leaving his wealthy and sophisticated homeland for a trek in a hostile desert would result in him becoming the father of God's chosen people. His was a decision which was *not supported by human reason*. God got into contact with Abraham, put inside him an ability to communicate with God and revealed His will to Abraham. Abraham, through *the faith factor*, entered a *new dimension*.

Abraham did not follow *the way that seemeth right unto man!*

There is no way that Noah could have worked out that a catastrophe such as had never been seen before and would never be seen again was going to engulf the earth.

Noah did not follow *the way that seemeth right unto man!*

There was no way that Moses could have recognised it to be better 'to suffer affliction with the people of God than to enjoy the pleasures of sin for a season'; the one would have seemed far more inviting to *human reason* than the other.

Moses did not follow *the way that seemeth right unto man!*

They were all recipients of *the faith factor*—the God-given *ability* to know God's will and the God-given *power* to do His will.

The God-given perception those men received could have come about in no other way than as a *supernatural* intervention in their lives by God Himself.

Knowing the will of God often resulted in these men

of faith shedding what human reasoning would tell them to do in favour of that which could only be discerned through *the inner voice*. The results which followed their actions of faith show that they had not moved to a lower plane of thought by adopting faith rather than reason but to a plane of perception which *transcends* reason.

I remember when we had steel gramophone needles—they came in boxes of several hundred because they had to be changed every two or so records. Now compact discs do not use needles at all; they use laser beams to read the disc. Because you can see no needle that does not mean that the manufacturer has taken leave of his senses but rather that he has moved to a higher plane of communication.

As we know, a bird or an animal with no visible means of navigation can navigate more accurately than most people with a map and a variety of instruments. Ultimately, though, even the instruments of navigation we humans use depend upon that which we cannot see, the influence of the magnetic pole and radar and radio waves.

A little thought will confirm to you that the most powerful influences known to man are those which cannot be seen.

There *is* another dimension—it is a dimension which will remain hidden from you until you have received *the faith factor*.

5 *The Invisible God*

I SAID IN A previous chapter that *you* have a problem. In this chapter I want to tell you that *God has a problem too!*

When the Apostle Paul visited Athens, he saw on Mars Hill a statue inscribed with the words 'To the unknown God' (Acts 17:23).

Now that does not mean that the Athenians were more ungodly than the rest of us as some would suppose. Perhaps they were more honest and merely following their overwhelming desire to pursue intellectual integrity.

The Athenians, at least, built their God of stone but one has the feeling that twentieth-century man would fashion his God in something akin to putty to be ever ready for change and infinitely malleable!

They could have done what many of us do or have done, that is, they could have *invented* a god and pretended that he was not unknown to them at all!

THE INVISIBLE GOD

Of course an invented god—the god we make in our own image—can give us great, if temporary, comfort because he *is* made in *our* image. He will be what we want him to be, behave in the way we want him to behave, support the causes we want him to support and pour convenient hatred on the things which do not fit our philosophy. Such a god will fit in with whatever morality is 'flavour of the month' and not impose embarrassing standards which are unfashionable.

Why do human beings imagine their own gods? The short answer is because the human mind is incapable of discerning the *real* God and, as someone once pointed out, man has such a spiritual need that if there is no god then man must invent one.

It is, one must admit, much more simple to erect an altar to 'The unknown God' or make an image of a god we think we know than to seek the real God who often seems to hide Himself from humankind.

If we strip away our conception of the god made in our own image and realise that God is not like us at all then we are in a better position to realise why God has to make contact with us in what we may regard as being a round-about-way.

God's problem

Yes, God has a problem!

Is it possible for you to wipe from your mind the vision of that old man who sits on the throne? God is *not* an old man who sits on a throne! Can you forget the god you have seen depicted in icon, painting and statue? God is not like any of them!

'No man hath seen God at any time' (John 1:18) the Bible declares and in another place it says, 'God is *a*

Spirit: and they that worship him must worship him in spirit and in truth' (John 4:24). No spirit is visible to the human eye though the *manifestation* of a spirit may be.

You will find it very difficult to know about God if you think of someone with two hands, two legs, two eyes and a nose. You will find it even more difficult to think of Him if you imagine Him as being three flesh-and-blood people with six hands, six legs and six eyes.

That is why the Bible says:

> Thou shalt make unto thyself no graven image, or likeness of any thing which is in heaven above, or on earth beneath; or that is in the water under the earth.
> Exodus 20:4

Make a plaster cast of God and you will destroy your appreciation of Him as being spirit, a different kind of being altogether from us. You will also create a credibility gap because immediately you conceive God as having a material form you will apply to Him the characteristics and limitations of solid matter.

That is God's problem—He cannot be seen by the human eye nor can He respond to any of the human senses. You cannot see Him, you cannot touch Him, taste Him, hear Him, or smell Him. The same applies to the spirit or spiritual world which He inhabits (if that is the correct term)—you cannot see it, touch it, taste it, hear it or smell it.

To become known to man God has had to *manifest* Himself and to make known the spiritual world to us He has had to *illustrate* it.

Remember those two words *'manifest'* and *'illustrate'* as we consider God and His spiritual world.

How can we believe in that which we cannot see?

It's very difficult! In fact we cannot properly do so without there being something, a link, between us and that which we cannot see—something that proves to us it is there. A simple illustration is an experiment every schoolboy knows—putting litmus paper into a liquid to see if it is acid. The paper changes colour and we know the effect is the result of a cause. The medium through which humankind can 'see' God is a special ability called 'faith'—it is the 'litmus paper' that reveals God.

Think of the force of gravity—it is invisible, we cannot see it and we cannot explain it but we know it is there because we see the effect and we know there must be a cause.

No one can *see* influence emanating from a magnet but we know when that influence is working because we see the *effect* it has on some metals. It is interesting in passing to note that magnetism will only attract certain metals and no other material! Materials with different qualities from those of magnetically responsive metals do not respond! Perhaps a fitting parable of how those with *the faith factor* are capable of responding to things spiritual while those without *the faith factor* are not!

The invisible influence

Have you got an infra-red programme changer facility on your television set?

If you have you will know that it enables you to sit some way from the television, point the unit at the set and change the programmes without actually touching the television set.

Now I have looked in vain to see if I could detect the infra-red beam passing from the hand control to the set.

I suggest *you* look carefully at your remote control unit the next time you operate it and try to see, hear, taste, touch or smell the influence which passes from the control unit to the set.

Of course you will see nothing, you will have no experience at all of the power which is passing from the control unit to the set. You could be forgiven for assuming that there was no influence passing from one to the other. But are we right to assume, because we cannot see the infra-red beam, that it is not there? Such an assumption would be ridiculous! Is it reasonable, in this modern age, to assume that because we cannot see, hear, touch, taste or smell something it does not exist?

Observe the radio-controlled toy. It moves this way and that at the command of the operator but there is no connection between the hand-set and the toy which we can comprehend with any of our five senses. Objects can be controlled, without a visible connection to the controlling source, by radio, over many miles. We are all too familiar with bombs being detonated by radio control.

It is now rather old fashioned, and unsustainable, to believe that invisible influences do not exist and that human experience is confined to the five senses. There was a time, when man was less advanced than now, that there was more reason to doubt the existence of anything which did not respond to our senses but it seems to me to be an untenable position now we know of so many unseen influences which exist and work for us in our everyday lives.

We *know* the infra-red beam is there because, though we cannot see, hear, touch, taste or smell it we can see what it does. It changes the picture on our television screen, it can change the colour tones, it can increase or decrease the volume and contrast. We know, without being too clever, that every *effect* has a *cause*. Though we cannot *see* it we know that if there was no influence or power passing from one to the other the phenomenon which we witness would not happen.

The radio waves which control a model boat, though unappreciated by any of our senses, can be shown to be there as surely as if we could see them, because of the effect they have upon the behaviour of the boat. The controller moves the controls and, without there being any visible attachment between the control unit and the boat, the boat moves in the way dictated by the controller.

The silent voice

The human mind strains at the 'spirit' concept of the supreme being, someone without eyes yet able to see, without ears and yet able to hear and without vocal chords and yet able to speak.

Yet ears and eyes are only two means by which messages may be received, and our vocal chords but one method of transmitting messages. There is evidence all around us that messages can be both received and transmitted by other means than by eyes, ears and vocal chords.

We know that many animals and plants are capable of receiving communications without them being audible in *our* sense of the word, and without bringing the normal organs of comprehension into play.

No migratory bird actually *hears* the vast voice of nature tell it to fly away to a preset destination at a certain time of the year and yet unerringly the voice of nature *does* speak to their inner selves, and millions of birds fly away punctually and accurately to climes they, as individuals, have never before visited and could not have known existed, travelling routes they have never before travelled! The *inner voice* invariably guides them to environments which are more suitable to them at certain times of the year. *The inexplicable inner voice proves to be more certain, more sure than their reasoning capabilities!*

A puffin was taken to Boston, USA, from its native habitat on the Welsh coast. Twelve days later, by its own volition, it arrived back in Wales. Its homeward voyage had involved flying a distance, mainly over water, of over 3,000 miles.

It was not a normal migratory journey, just as the homeward flights of homing pigeons are not normal migratory journeys. Had the bird flown the outward journey, one may have assumed, however unlikely the assumption, that a computer-like memory had guided the bird back to its native land. Had, on the other hand, the journey been part of a repetitious pattern of migration one could have assumed the journey to have been connected with some kind of 'instinct' or 'genetic inheritance'.

What *caused* that bird to return and what *enabled* it to return?

Perhaps you will consider that if there is a compulsion for certain birds to return home then there is also a compulsion, *the faith factor,* within human beings which can guide them back to God.

We are all familiar with the migration of birds, but perhaps, less so with the migratory habits of other species in the animal kingdom.

Consider the European eel

The European eel, for example, has been known to pass over land to obey its migratory impulse. It migrates from its native waters to far-away waters in an area to the south-west of Bermuda. Despite many pseudo-scientific words—used mainly to disguise a lack of knowledge—no one has yet produced a satisfactory explanation as to how or why the eel is motivated to make the journey.

The eel sets out on the journey not knowing *why* and not knowing *whither* it is bound. The whole process is above and beyond its powers of reason just as *the faith factor* which caused Abraham to leave Ur of the Chaldees and journey to he knew not where was above and beyond reason. Yes there *is* a higher voice!

A Danish scientist, Johannes Schmidt, has discovered that the American eel breeds in an area overlapping the area in which the British eel breeds. At one time it was thought that the return of the eel to its own waters was merely a matter of 'drifting' with the prevailing current. Now, however, we know that the larva of the American eel returns to American waters and the larva of the British eel returns to British waters and that despite the fact that they have been thoroughly 'mixed up' in the same area. Certainly it seems to be more a result of an inner urge than of 'drifting'. Perhaps we can think of that as an illustration of what *the faith factor* is all about!

The migratory instinct of the Alaskan fur seal

The Alaskan fur seal breeds only near the Pribilof Islands in the Bering Sea and then returns to Southern California, a distance of 3,000 miles, until it migrates again the following spring. An obvious motivating force would be the search for a warmer environment, but if that were so then why should they return to the, always colder, waters of the Arctic? In any case, how do they know where to go and find the environment they desire?

Can you really imagine a seal reasoning to himself, 'The water here will be getting unbearably cold in the next few months, let us away to Southern California where the water is much warmer'? Of course not! When migration time comes around they get an inner urge to do that which proves to be right. As did Abraham, they, not knowing why, head directly for the place the 'inner voice' instructs them to go.

The mystery of the Monarch butterfly

One of the most astounding instances of the silent voice in action is to be seen in the migration of the Monarch butterfly. Each year it leaves the North of the United States and migrates to lay its eggs.

The parent butterflies die, the young hatch and they return to the *exact* area of the United States from which their parents originally came.

Perhaps the most eerie part of the story is that on the southward journey the parents use certain trees on which to alight, and, on the homeward journey, the progeny use exactly the same flight path and alight on exactly the same trees as their parents used on the outward journey. Scientists have sought in vain to discover why one tree should be chosen on both the flight out and the flight back whilst other trees, identical in every respect, are not used.

False limitations on human experience

Perhaps we are being restrictive when we think of the human being for ever limited within its present bounds. There seems no reason why, if certain birds, seals, eels and butterflies are able to be motivated by an *inner voice* that other birds do not hear, certain people should not be guided by an *inner voice* which other people do not comprehend.

Consider the crocus bulb. It is dormant until it is instructed by nature to spring forth. Why do trees bud in the spring, blossom in the summer and lose their leaves in the autumn? There *is* a voice, not spoken with the mouth, not heard with the ears, it's true, but a voice none-the-less which communicates.

Some shrink from discussing such possibilities in human beings and that is to be understood because one feels either arrogant in the presence of the inexplicable or, on the other hand, too humble at the grandness of it all. On the one hand we may say, 'I insult my intelligence by seeking after that which may not exist', and on the other, 'Who am I that I should perceive that which others have failed to perceive.' We should be neither too arrogant nor too humble to seek. There is nothing at all foolish about trying to push the boundaries of one's experience beyond what they are at a given time—that is the stuff of which *all* human progress is made.

Even Charles Darwin believed in the creator

You see, though we often try very hard not to do so, we, most of us, believe that there is *always* a cause and effect. We are not inclined to believe for one moment that a teacup of even the simplest design came about by chance and even Charles Darwin did not believe, as is often alleged, that the universe was made without God's intervention.

Darwin wrote in his book *The Origin of Species*, 'Therefore I should refer from analogy that probably all living things which have ever lived upon this earth have descended from one primordial into which life was first *breathed by the creator*.'

Unfortunately, by the time evolution had arrived among the 'blackboard scientists' on the classroom floor, it had been turned into a charter for the atheist and agnostic. Darwin did not intend it to be that; he saw nothing in his theory of evolution which lessened the need for belief in a *thinking first cause*.

The Great Universal Spirit

The Bible tells us that God is a Spirit and that, by definition, makes Him the Great Universal Spirit.

> God is a Spirit: and they that worship him must worship him in spirit and in truth.   John 4:24

That presents a difficulty to the human mind because a spirit, rather like magnetism, gravity, the infra-red beam on our television programme changer or the radio wave which controls a model, cannot be seen. Neither does a spirit respond to our touch, our taste, our sense of smell or our hearing. No one has ever *seen* a spirit because a spirit is not visible.

Now look at the meaning of the word 'manifestation' in your dictionary. One definition is 'a revelation of'.

Though God is a Spirit and we cannot see a spirit, that is *not* to say that no man has ever seen a *manifestation* of

THE INVISIBLE GOD

a spirit nor that no man has ever seen a *manifestation* of God.

Some people like to ask trick questions such as 'What language does God speak?' or 'What does God look like?' The answer is that when God speaks, He is manifesting Himself and He speaks the language of those to whom He is manifesting Himself at the time. When God appears He is manifesting Himself and He appears in whatever form is most likely to achieve the purpose of His manifestation at that time.

A spirit has no earthly language and I must confess that I have no idea how one spirit communicates with another spirit. A spirit has no skin so it is not black or white, it is not born anywhere so it has no ethnic origin, it has no body so it has no standard form of clothing, it is not male or female. All this applies to God who is—*a Spirit*.

A problem of communication

You will appreciate the problem God has, right away. How does something which does not respond to our sense of sight, sound, touch, taste or smell communicate with us?

Take a little time to think about, or meditate upon, that and then you will understand why God has to do things in certain ways which, at first, may seem unnecessary and irrational. You will soon come to appreciate that, what at first may seem an involved game which God is playing with human beings, is, in fact, an essential process if we are to know anything about Him.

Until God reveals Himself to us there is hardly an experience of human life which relates to Him. His world no more relates to our world and experience than our world and its goings on are explicable to a goldfish. There are so many things we do *not* know and our experience of the world of spirit is almost nil.

A half-hour appreciation test

Don't just read on—I really want you to take half an hour and think deeply about how you, if *you* did not respond to any of the five human senses, would communicate with other people. You'd have to think of some way in which you could *manifest* yourself to them. Probably you would not find a way to let them know all about you but at least you would be able to establish a level of communication.

Even if you were trying to communicate with people whose five senses did respond to you but were of a very different culture you would find it difficult.

Here is a half-hour appreciation test. Think for a while about God's problem. You will appreciate His problem in communicating with us if you imagine you are confronted by someone who has lived their whole life away from civilisation.

How would you explain central heating to such a person if they have never seen a house? How would you describe a Boeing 707 to them? How would you describe a motor car with a turbo charged engine? How would you describe a neutron?

The answer is, of course, that you would start by relating those things to things they have experienced. You may liken the Boeing 707 to a bird. That would not be sufficient, though, because you would have to explain that the bird had to 'drink' a lakeful of a fiery liquid before it could fly. You would have to explain too that it could carry hundreds of people in its belly.

THE INVISIBLE GOD

If your listener was a particularly naive kind of person he might go back and literalise what you had said and then he would miss the spirit of what you were telling him. If he became over-dogmatic about it he might well be just as much in the dark *after* you had explained as he was before. He would create a great debate on how there could possibly be such a large bird, how much blood flowed through its veins, the colour of its feathers, the size of its beak, how big it was when it hatched from the egg and what happened to such a body mass when the bird died.

Of course, literalised in that way, the whole thing would become quite ridiculous and few but the most credulous would find it possible to believe in the 'bird'. Yet you and I know that that 'bird' *does*, in its essential teaching, exist. There are thousands of things which fly, have wings, consume fuel by the thousands of gallons and carry hundreds of people in their 'belly' from one place to another. All that is *fact*; it is the pushing of the simile beyond its legitimate use and to its extreme that causes the confusion.

Imagine that the people of whom we are thinking do not live near the sea, they have never seen the sea or heard about it, the sea is something which is entirely outside of their experience. Now try to describe a submarine to those people, try to tell them what it is and what it does. A great fish in the belly of which a hundred men can live? 'Ah,' they laugh, 'but no such things could swim in the shallow waters of our lake,' and so starts yet another 'theological' argument! Try telling them that this fish feeds the men for months and swims for months without eating. Tell them that great fish has a sting which it can shoot into the sky and which will destroy whole cities. A fish that could—well I'm sure you will see how difficult it all is!

The 'word pictures' of the Bible

The first thing you would have to do if you were trying to explain civilisation to someone who had not experienced it would be to establish a medium of communication. God did just that and Paul writing to Timothy says:

> From a child thou hast known the holy scriptures, which are able to make thee wise unto salvation through faith which is in Christ Jesus. *All scripture is given by inspiration of God,* and is profitable for doctrine, for reproof, for correction, for instruction in righteousness. 2 Timothy 3:15,16

I want you to accept for the moment my proposition that the Bible is the Word of God.

Think of what a word is. It's a way in which we express our thoughts one to another. A word is a method by which we reveal our hopes and desires to other people. We can also make ourselves known by our facial expressions and in other physical ways but because 'No man hath seen God at any time' there is no way in which God can make His revelation known to us other than by His Word.

The Bible is the written Word of God and Jesus Christ was the living Word of God. Now read what John said about the living Word.

> In the beginning was the Word, and the Word was with God, and the Word was God.
> The same was in the beginning with God.

All things were made by him; and without him was not anything made that was made.

In him was life; and the life was the light of men.

And the light shineth in the darkness; and the darkness comprehended it not...

That was the true Light, which lighteth every man that cometh into the world.

He was in the world, and the world was made by him, and the world knew him not.

He came unto his own, and his own received him not.

But as many as received him, *to them gave he power to become the sons of God...*

Who were born, not of blood, nor of the will of the flesh, nor of the will of man, but of God.

And *the Word was made flesh,* and dwelt among us (and we beheld his glory as of the only begotten of the Father), full of grace and truth.

John 1:1–5, 9–14

Paul, the Apostle, wrote:

God who at sundry times and in divers manners spoke in time past unto the fathers by the prophets, *hath in these last days spoke unto us by his Son, whom he hath appointed heir of all things, by whom* also he made the worlds.

Hebrews 1:1–2

God manifest in the flesh

Just as the Bible is the *written Word* so the Lord Jesus Christ is *the living Word*. Following on to the manifestations of God in the Old Testament, God became manifest in the flesh and dwelt amongst us.

It was an event for which God had been conditioning mankind from the foundation of the world. Paul describes what had gone before:

> The law was a schoolmaster to bring us unto Christ, that we might be justified by faith.   Galatians 3:24

There are indeed many valuable lessons to be learned from the Old Testament before we can fully appreciate the New Testament. As someone once said, 'The New is in the Old concealed and the Old is in the New revealed.'
The Apostle Paul tells us:

> For the law, having a *shadow* of good things to come and not the very image of the things, can never with those sacrifices which they offered year by year continually make those who come to it perfect.   Hebrews 10:1

We are told too that the Old Testament contains 'The example and *shadow* of heavenly things' (Hebrews 8:5) and 'The *patterns* of things in the heavens' (Hebrews 9:23) and '*a shadow of things to come;* but the substance is of Christ' (Colossians 2:17).

The unknown God

Most people have little doubt about the *existence* of a god of sorts. They have a fairly ill-formed idea that there is 'something up there' or some kind of 'supreme being' or, as the Athenians put it, 'The Unknown God'.

We look around us and see a marvellous and intricate creation and it takes a great deal of credulity to believe other than that creation demands there be a creator.

THE INVISIBLE GOD

It is basic to our thinking that we consider even the simplest form of design, whether it be a cave painting or simple piece of pottery, to be evidence that some thinking being has passed that way. Would someone propose that even a simple triangle chiselled into a rock had come there by chance?

That much is fairly obvious because we know that nothing happens either by chance or by the law of averages. There could be no science of any kind if that were not so! That earth and everything upon it is governed by the laws of nature is self-evident. *Everything* happens according to law.

Much is made by some, who would wish to explain away the fairly obvious fact that creation must have had a creator, of the power of chance and the law of averages to determine things. In fact neither does determine things!

Consider whether, if you put a million heavy stones in your back garden, one of them would jump ten feet into the air by chance or through the law of averages. Of course, none of them would! If you put a million tadpoles into your garden pond, how many of them would by chance or the law of averages turn into anything but a frog? Put a million kettles at the North Pole, leave them there for a thousand years and consider how many of them would boil by chance or because the law of averages demands that one of them does so.

We sometimes consider, wrongly, that a law has been set aside, when, what has actually happened is that another law which is, for the time being, exerting a stronger influence has taken over. When an aeroplane leaves the runway, the law of gravity is not abolished; it is overcome by the law of aerodynamics which, by reason of cause and effect, is at that time in the ascendancy.

Think again of what Charles Darwin said when he affirmed God as being the first cause and reflect upon the fact that all science is based upon the affirmation that invariable laws exist and that nothing happens by chance.

Oh yes! There is plenty of evidence for the existence of 'a one above' or an *unknown god* but that is not the quest we have undertaken. Our quest is quite different, it is for the *one true and ever-living God*. We cannot arrive at a knowledge of Him through human observation or human reason.

The written Word—the living Word

The purpose of the whole Bible both Old and New Testaments (the written Word) and of the coming of Jesus Christ (the living Word) is to reveal the *unknown God* to man. Both make comprehensible that which is otherwise incomprehensible.

To sum up this chapter: we see that God is a Spirit and we know that a spirit does not respond to any of our five senses. We cannot see it, taste it, touch it, smell it or hear it.

We have seen that God *has* manifested Himself to humanity firstly through the Bible and then through the coming of Jesus Christ.

To understand what God has revealed about Himself we must avoid overliteralisation. Often He uses natural similes to illustrate eternal truths. We must not press these 'word pictures' beyond the point of truth.

There *is* only one way in which we can come to know God and that is through the revelation of God Himself to us. He has revealed Himself through the Bible and He has revealed Himself in Jesus Christ.

Jesus said:

> Unless a man be born again, he cannot *see* the kingdom of God. John 3:3

Read carefully the context of that saying for it is the very basis of the Christian faith.

Note the precise words '*cannot see*'. Some misconstrue what Jesus said by teaching that it means that unless a man is born again he cannot *enter* the kingdom of God. What it says is that unless a man is born again he cannot *see* the kingdom of God.

It is only through the 'new birth' that we can understand, appreciate and perceive the kingdom of God, otherwise it is invisible to us and not discernible by us.

In another chapter we will see how it is possible to *enter that new dimension* which Jesus called the 'new birth'.

6 Whosoever will may come

THERE IS, always has been and always will be a great debate around the question of human free will and predestination. It is a debate that need not concern us here because the Bible says that *'whosoever* shall call upon the name of the Lord shall be saved' (Acts 2:21). Back of all the argument and debate there is that unqualified promise—*whosoever* shall call upon the name of the Lord *shall* be saved!

The question then is *will you?* Do you have the *'will'* to come?

Whatever the theology of the matter, the practicality of the matter is that if you *will* come to a knowledge of God then you *can* come to a knowledge of God and if you *do not will* to come to a knowledge of God then *you will* not come to a knowledge of God.

Your personalised invitation to experience the new dimension

An invitation addressed to *the whosoever* is the most personal invitation it is possible to receive!

My name is more unusual than most—there are not as many Victor Dunstans as there are Tom Browns about. Yet a few evenings ago the telephone rang and the caller said, 'Is that Victor Dunstan?' When I answered in the affirmative the caller said, 'Do you remember me? We were in the Eighth Army together in the Western Desert. I've been thinking of looking you up for years but I never got round to it. I found your name and number in the telephone directory.'

I told him that I would have been very honoured to have served in the Eighth Army but I was far too young at the time the war in the Western Desert was raging. 'Well,' he said, 'I am sorry to have troubled you but when I saw your name in the telephone book I thought there couldn't be anyone else with *that name* around here so I rang.'

Obviously there is, or was, a Victor Dunstan who lived in my neck of the woods and served with the Eighth Army.

The point is that to be addressed by your name can be a case of mistaken identity! It is not nearly as personal as being addressed as one of the 'whosoever'! The word 'whosoever' means that *not one* human being is left out. It is an invitation more surely personalised to you than if someone addressed the invitation to you and put your own name on it! However unique your name there are sure to be a lot of other people with the same name and there is always the possibility that the invitation was intended for someone else.

You have received an invitation addressed to the

'whosoever' and there can be no mistaken identity for, whoever you might or might not be, whatever your address, whatever your nationality, whatever your religion, no matter what you have or have not done during your life—you are most surely one of the whosoever!

The most inclusive word in any language has been used by the greatest authority and most reliable keeper of promises in the universe to tell you *you are personally invited into the kingdom of heaven*—isn't that marvellous?

The gift is free but you will have to collect it

We have seen that Christianity is a *revealed religion* and that you need the gift of *faith* from God before you can have an experience with God.

That is the purpose of our next step—to ask God for the gift of *faith* so that you can discern the things of God.

Don't worry if at this moment you are still more than a little incredulous about the claims and doctrine of the Christian faith—that is, as I have said, quite natural. I am at this point going to ask you to take a step in the dark, an experimental step and ask God for the gift of faith.

Let us look more closely at what God instructs us to do and how He promises He will respond:

> Ask, and it shall be given unto you; seek, and ye shall find; knock, and it shall be opened unto you. For everyone that asketh receiveth; and he that seeketh findeth; and to him that knocketh it shall be opened. Luke 11:9,10

Promise 1: Ask and it shall be given unto you

The first thing you have to do then is to *ask* for guidance. Asking God for things is one aspect of what we call *prayer*.

As I have said, even if you cannot bring yourself to believe that God exists take the experimental step of praying to the God who *might exist*. There is nothing foolish about this. Every scientist and every logician knows the value of working from a hypothesis, or, as the dictionary defines the word, 'A supposition made as a basis for reasoning without reference to its truth, or as a starting point for investigation.'

You may receive the revelation in an instant, all your doubts will vanish and you will wonder why you have not believed before. I have known that to happen to many thousands of people, some of them very 'worldly-wise' people indeed.

Do not be disheartened if nothing happens the first time you pray. There is a 'word picture' in the Bible which I hope you will read (Genesis 30:24–32), about Jacob wrestling with an angel. He wrestled all night and said, 'I will not let you go unless you bless me.' That is the kind of earnestness and persistence that brings God's blessing. Unfortunately many of us have been indoctrinated with the belief that we only have to pray and we will be 'served' rather more quickly than we would be served at a supermarket counter.

I watched a rugby training film a few days ago and I was impressed by the sheer dedication of the young men who play for the national sides of France, England, Ireland, Scotland and Wales. One young man, who was typical of them all, told how he spent every evening of the week except Friday and Sunday training for two or three hours. How many people allocate even one hour a week to their search for God?

People study for years to learn to play the piano, or perhaps I should say these days 'the keyboard'. No one would think for one moment that they could walk onto a football field and be competent at the game in a few minutes. Yet people often close their eyes for a minute or so and wonder why they have not had a profound experience of God!

First realise that you cannot take the second two steps 'seeking' and 'knocking' until you have asked and received. Remember that you are not asking God a question or a series of questions, you are asking God to do something *to* you and *for* you. You are asking God to put within you *the faith factor*, the missing part, so that you have the *ability* to tune in to Him.

Obtain a Bible and turn to the scriptures that I have quoted. Accept experimentally for the moment that the Bible is God's Word and that through its pages He is speaking directly to you.

Now read Peter's confession of faith:

> When Jesus came into the coasts of Caesarea Philippi, he asked his disciples, saying, Whom do men say that I the Son of man am? And they said, Some say that thou art John the Baptist; some Elijah; and others, Jeremiah, or one of the prophets. He said unto them, But who say ye that I am? And Simon Peter answered and said, Thou art the Christ, the Son of the living God. And Jesus answered and said unto him, Blessed art thou, Simon Bar-jona: *for flesh and blood hath not revealed it unto thee, but my Father who is in heaven.* Matthew 16:13–16

Here is the same point driven home once more by Jesus Himself. Peter could not have obtained the ability to *know who Jesus was* unless it had been directly revealed to him by God the Father.

If you follow God's instruction suddenly a new spiritual perception will come to you

You first step is to organise a quiet room where you will not be disturbed and be prepared to meditate on the Scriptures and upon what you are asking God to do.

If you are an average sort of person you have probably often prayed, especially in times of bereavement, illness or fear. Now you are going to ask God to do something quite different, you are going to ask Him to reveal Himself to you!

Pray something like this: 'Lord I have read in your Word your promise: "Ask and it shall be given unto you, seek and you will find, knock and it will be opened for you." I have read Peter's confession of faith. I know that flesh and blood cannot reveal your truths to me but I ask you that, as you did with Peter, so you will reveal the deep eternal truths about yourself to me.'

Sometimes in an instant but always with persistence you will receive your 'new part'—*the faith factor*. Suddenly the scriptures you have read will come to mind spontaneously—you will have entered into a new world of perception. You will have become aware of God.

Faith is not something a person can generate within themselves; it comes from outside of ourselves—it is 'not of yourselves, it is a gift of God'.

How then do we receive this gift of faith? 'Ask and *it* shall be given unto you.' The *'it'* in that promise is *'faith'*. Without that faith you cannot comprehend God or the things of God; with that faith you can no more doubt God than you can doubt your own existence.

At the end of your little prayer sessions you will probably hear no audible voice speaking to you, but while you are 'asking' your spiritual eyes will be opened and your soul will 'see' Jesus in all His glory. You will say with Saint Peter, 'Thou art the Christ the Son of the living God.' A voice within you will reply, 'Blessed art thou (your name) for flesh and blood hath not revealed it to you but my Father which is in heaven.'

Promise 2: Seek and you will find

At the same time you commence your *asking* begin your *seeking*. Now 'seeking' is different from 'asking' as you will realise.

You *seek* when you know that there is something which is hidden from your view. We seek for something by following clues as to where it may be. If, for example, you can't find the keys for your car you may try to think where they were when you last saw them. That may give you a clue to where they may be now.

There are several ways you can *seek*. The first and very important way is by reading the Bible. Continue to read and meditate upon some of the quotations I have given in this book. I say 'meditate' because it is not sufficient to give them only a cursory reading—each verse has a much deeper meaning than can be explored by superficial reading, each verse contains vital, eternal truth!

Ask the right people

Another way you can seek something which is lost is to ask *people who might know* the whereabouts of that which you seek. Obviously you will not ask people who do not have a reason to know where that for which you are looking is. You wouldn't, for example, walk up to the first person you met in the street and ask, 'Do you know where I left my car keys?'

If you think that is ridiculous then I would suggest that it is no more ridiculous than the national magazine, it shall remain nameless, which asked one hundred surgeons what they believed about life after death. As one would expect the surgeons, being intelligent fellows, replied that their training as surgeons gave them no more nor less knowledge of the afterlife than anyone else.

Pontius Pilate is among the many people who have made the mistake of asking the *wrong people* what he should do with Jesus (John 18:39). He would have received a very different answer if he had asked the people who had been touched and healed by Jesus! If you ask the wrong question of the wrong people then you are sure to get the wrong answer.

Make sure *you* ask the *right people*. Who are the right people? They are the people who were once in your present situation—those who sought and found.

Where will you find such people?

You will find them in some of your local churches but not in *all* your local churches.

How will you know in which churches to find them?

The churches in which you will find active Christians and ministers prepared to help you in your search are known as 'evangelical' or 'fundamentalist' churches, though they may not have either of those words in their name. There are evangelical and fundamentalist churches in most denominations.

Now I must warn you that no church, minister or Christian is perfect but they *will* be able to help you in your search. Do not use them as your *example*, your one example is Jesus Himself. *All* we Christians fall short of that example but, despite our shortcomings, we *can* help to guide you along the way. Speaking for myself, I pray that you will become a better Christian than I have managed to be.

If you cannot find an evangelical or fundamentalist church in your area then find a Christian bookshop and ask them—they will be pleased to help you. When you find a church please contact the minister and tell him that you are obeying Christ's injunction to *'seek'*. He will be very pleased to help you and he will introduce you to people who will also be pleased to help you. As a bonus, you'll make a lot of good friends.

Don't just wander into a church and sit down. Despite the newspaper advertisements 'A warm welcome extended to all', public relations is still not one of the church's strong points, consequently, in some churches, you will be left to come and go without anyone introducing themselves.

Even the churches that are enthusiastic about extending a 'welcoming hand' do not generally these days engage in 'buttonholing' people. You will find that they respect your privacy and that may lead you to think that they don't care. They *do* care but they are often as timid as you are. So tell the minister who you are and tell him how he can help you—you'll find him, or her, very friendly and helpful.

When you go to a doctor's surgery with a medical problem you *ask* to see the doctor and when you go to church with a spiritual problem you should ask to see the minister. You will find that ministers are not only willing but eager to help and most members of their congregation will be friendly and helpful too.

Listen to the preacher

It's surprising how many ministers now apologise for preaching. 'Now I don't intend to preach to you this evening' or 'I never preach to anyone' are often-used phrases. The implication is that they are going to *talk* to people rather than *preach* to them.

I wonder why preaching has fallen into such disuse? Preaching is an indispensable part of the Christian message.

The Bible says:

> For whosoever shall call upon the name of the Lord shall be saved. How then shall they call on him in whom they have not believed? And how shall they believe in him of whom they have not heard? And how shall they hear without a *preacher*? And how shall they preach, unless they be sent?
> Romans 10:13,14 and 15

The difference between someone talking and someone preaching is that talking is something we can do from human reasoning but preaching is God's method of conveying enlightenment through a preacher who has not only been given a message to deliver but also been given a unique power to deliver it. 'And how shall they preach unless they are sent?' Preaching is not something to be despised; it is God's method, a Holy Spirit-inspired way of conveying His Word to the world.

The Bible reinforces this by saying:

> For after that, in the wisdom of God, *the world by wisdom knew not God,* it pleased God *by the foolishness of preaching* to save them that believed.
> 1 Corinthians 1:20,21

That is not to say that preachers are always good men or as men always good—you are exhorted to listen to the preacher not because there is any innate goodness in him but because he is an instrument, chosen of God and used of God, to proclaim God's message.

You may learn from the media sometimes of the regrettable failures of some preachers. Don't let that disturb you—it's nothing new! The Bible recognises that the lives of some preachers leave a lot to be desired when it says:

> Some, indeed, preach Christ even of envy and strife; and some also of goodwill: the one preach Christ of contention, not sincerely, supposing to add affliction to my bonds; but the other of love, knowing that I am set for the defence of the gospel. What then? Notwithstanding, every way, whether in pretence, or in truth, *Christ is preached;* and in that I do rejoice.
> Philippians 1:15–18

It is the message that is sacred, not the man!

Promise 3: Knock and it shall be opened to you

'Knock and it shall be opened unto you,' Jesus said. You don't knock on a door if you have the key. Once again we have emphasised that human beings do not have the key to open the door which leads to God.

Only the Holy Spirit can unlock the door of the knowledge of God. The past several decades have seen a dramatic increase in learning which is, of course, to be encouraged. Unfortunately, though, there is also the feeling among some that their education in some way puts them beyond the 'simple faith' which stood their fathers in such good stead—a clear case of looking for stars through a microscope!

As I have said, I am a great believer in human progress and I think people should seek all the knowledge available to them as long as they keep the things of God in perspective. They should not confuse the telescope with the microscope and use the wrong instrument for the wrong purpose.

No degree in mathematics, medicine, law, history, science or any other subject, not even theology, will give anyone more ability than a road digger to know about the things of God. I happen to have made several millions of pounds in my lifetime but I don't know any more about God because of that. Sometimes I think that all I know about God I know *despite* that! All I know about God I know because I knocked on the *correct door* and, as Jesus promised, it was opened to me.

None of my learning, none of whatever ability I might have, none of my understanding of financial matters and none of my reading of history imparted to me the slightest knowledge of God. All I know about God came through revelation, the revelation contained in the Bible and made to live in my life by the workings of the Holy Spirit.

Read and re-read the following scripture until you know it by heart:

> For the preaching of the cross is to them that perish foolishness; but unto us that are saved it is the power of God. For it is written, I will destroy the wisdom of the wise, and will bring to nothing the understanding of the prudent. Where is the wise? Where is the scribe? Where is the disputer of this age? Hath God not made foolish the wisdom of this world?
> 1 Corinthians 1:18–20

That is not meant to pour scorn on learning, it is meant merely to put it in its place. The historian knows about history, the medical man knows about medicine, the accountant knows about finance, the lawman knows about law but when it comes to knowing about God their learning in those things is of no help to them.

As I soon came to realise, the knowledge of God is not to be found in a financial textbook nor in the wisest tome on property development. No, the Apostle Paul, the writer of the above scripture, was no despiser of learning; he was himself a scholar and an intellectual but he recognised that 'Natural man discerneth not the things of God' and that, essential as learning is, it is no substitute for the preaching of the cross in the power of the Holy Spirit. Paul spent a considerable part of his life learning about things but not knowing about God—knowing about God had to come by revelation.

I give you every encouragement to knock on the door of learning and, walking through it, you will be faced with many wonderful things which will enrich your life. I beseech you to knock on the door of culture because through it you will come to enjoy gracious living, majestic music, great paintings, good literature and the fine and noble things of life. I would urge you to knock on the door of success, for there is no inherent virtue in failure and you deserve to experience the wonderful satisfaction of achievement. The one thing you must not do is think that any of those things will bring you one iota closer to God.

It stands to reason doesn't it that if you knock on the wrong door you will meet the wrong person.

Jesus said:

> I am *the* door: by me if any man enter in, he shall be saved.   John 10:9

Whichever the door on which you knock you will experience whatever is the other side of it. There are many wonderful experiences to be legitimately had in life which are non-Christian—that's quite different from being unChristian—but none of them is as enriching, confidence-evoking and satisfying as an experience with God. You will not be able to experience what is on the other side of *that* door until it is opened to you by He who has the key.

Despite what some would have us believe, and at the risk of being thought to be dogmatic, I will draw your attention to the fact that Jesus is the only doorway into the presence of God. Here are some more words of Jesus:

> I am *the* way, the truth, and *the* life: no man cometh unto the Father, but by *me*.   John 14:6

You have the solemn promise of Jesus Himself that if you ask you will receive, if ye seek then you will find and if you knock it shall be opened to you.

7 *A promise from God to you*

JESUS SAID, 'He that heareth my word, and believeth on him that sent me, hath everlasting life, and shall not come into condemnation; but *is* passed from death unto life' (John 5:24).

In a previous chapter I have quoted the Bible when it says, 'Natural man receiveth not the things of the Spirit of God; for they are foolishness unto him; neither can he know them, because they are *spiritually discerned*' (1 Corinthians 2:14).

Now I would like to quote another scripture which emphasised that point:

> Eye hath not seen, nor ear heard, neither have entered into the heart of man, the things which God hath prepared for them that love him.
>
> 1 Corinthians 2:9

Read again the scripture (1 Corinthians 1:18) which

A PROMISE FROM GOD TO YOU

tells us that 'the preaching of the cross is to those who perish foolishness'.

I have said that the only way it is possible for the spiritually dead to live, the spiritually blind to see and the spiritually deaf to hear is by them receiving the 'missing part'—*the faith factor* as a gift from God.

Faith, we have seen, is available by asking God for it, or, to use a religious word, 'praying' for it. We read the promise of Jesus that everyone who asks receives, everyone who seeks finds and everyone who knocks upon the door of eternal knowledge has that door opened.

If you have fulfilled those three requirements you will now be eager to progress further and the promise of Jesus quoted at the commencement of this chapter will be interesting and meaningful to you. If, however, the preaching of the cross is still 'foolishness' to you and the promise at the beginning of this chapter does not excite you then you should return to the chapter on asking, seeking and finding and re-read it.

If you read on beyond this point I am going to assume that, in response to your request, you now feel a responsiveness to the things of God and are beginning to feel a conviction that the way you have lived your life in the past has been unsatisfactory both from YOUR point of view and God's. If you have that feeling, that is a proof that you have that 'missing part'—*the faith factor*—working within you.

At first you will begin to feel the need for a closer relationship with God and you will find yourself becoming ever more interested in spiritual things. The things you once thought of no account will have become very important in your life. That is the first evidence that you have ceased to be spiritually dead, blind and deaf.

You may feel badly about your past life, though

previously you thought it to be rather admirable, and *that* is what is called, in religious terminology, 'conviction of sin'; it is the way in which God causes you to go forward to a higher level of spiritual experience.

Switch on to God

To continue our television simile—you have got your 'new part' and now is the time to switch your set on to receive the new station, a station you could not have received without the 'new part'. Later, after you have switched on, we will think of you 'tuning in'.

The promise of Jesus quoted at the beginning of this chapter is that if you HEAR His word and BELIEVE on Him that sent Him you will have everlasting life. Let us look at that promise.

Eternal life—here and now

Three very important words in that promise are the words *'hath'* (it means 'has got') and *'is passed'*; they are important because they are in the present tense.

There are just two conditions you have to fulfil, and immediately you fulfil them you will *know* that you *have got* everlasting life. There is no qualification which overrides Jesus' plain promise to you, no 'perhaps', 'maybe' or 'possibly'. You do not have to look to some time in the future when you will pass from death unto life—the new, everlasting life begins here and now.

I once asked someone if he believed in life after death and he replied miserably, 'I don't even believe in life *before* death.' Of course he was joking, not being able to resist the opportunity of a little repartee and perhaps being a little bit under the weather from the night before!

The answer is that there is a life, as distinct from an existence, before death. Jesus said that when you comply with His two conditions you *at that moment* pass from death unto life. It is a new kind of life, a different *quantity* of life, a different *quality* of life, a different *dimension* of life, everlasting life, and it begins in the here and now!

The Apostle Peter described the life *before death* in Jesus as being 'Joy *unspeakable* and full of glory' (1 Peter 1:8)—can you at this moment honestly describe your life as being full of joy unspeakable and full of glory? If not then you are missing out on the quality of life you could enjoy.

Paul in his letter to the Philippians speaks of 'The peace of God which passeth all understanding' (Philippians 4:7). Can you honestly tell yourself that you are so at peace with yourself that you can describe that peace as being the peace of God which passeth all understanding? If not then you are missing out on the quality of life you could enjoy.

Take it from me, there are not words to describe the ecstatic experience of *life in the new dimension* nor can anyone who has not experienced it know the utter peace of living in Jesus Christ. That's what caused the old Yorkshire Christian to tell an enquirer, 'Eee' lad, it's better felt than telt.'

I am quite sure that most people are completely unaware that there is any other area of perception than the one which they have experienced from the time that they were born. Undoubtedly a man who is blind from birth is incapable of knowing, except in so far as other people tell him, that there are experiences beyond his own experience.

The opening of the 'spiritual eyes' is an experience which, anyone who has experienced it will tell you, is the most momentous thing which can happen to a person in this life.

Hearing and harkening

Jesus gave two conditions for receiving everlasting life: they were 'He that *heareth* my word and *believeth* on him that sent me'—hearing and believing.

You may think that both are simple conditions and that you have complied with them already but you are probably wrong. Though they seem simple there is a lot more to them than at first appears.

We hear a lot of things we don't harken to! By that I mean we hear a lot of things we do not take notice of.

My old schoolmaster used to roar in a voice which was a fair impression of a cross between an Aberdeen Angus and a sergeant major, 'Do you hear what I say boy?' Of course we heard, everything he said was an assault on the eardrums, but that was not what he meant; he was not asking us if we heard the sound of his voice, he meant 'are you listening', 'are you paying attention', 'are you harkening to me'. That is precisely what Jesus meant when He said, 'He that heareth'.

There were many in Jesus' day who stood around Him when He was speaking and heard His words; some accepted His words and others rejected them. Quite obviously Jesus did *not* mean that by the physical act of hearing words *they* would inherit everlasting life. Those who *accepted* His words did receive everlasting life, those who did not accept His words did not receive everlasting life, but they *all* physically heard His words.

So when Jesus spoke of you 'hearing' His word He meant *accepting* His word, *paying attention to* His word.

My first question to you then is:

Are you prepared to accept the Word of God?

If you have followed the process of asking-seeking-knocking you will find the next step, *accepting,* to be an easy thing to do because you will now have the *missing part—the faith factor*—which will enable you to discern the things of God. You may have read your Bible from childhood without it ever changing your life but it *will* change your life this time because you are now *God responsive.*

Here are the things Jesus asks you to accept, and you *will* accept them because you now know that the knowledge of God comes by revealed religion not by human appreciation:

The Bible describes the natural condition of all men— will you accept it!

The Bible describes the *natural* condition of man:

> But the scriptures hath concluded *all* under sin, that the promise by faith of Jesus Christ might be given to them that believe. Galatians 3:22

Some people think that if you do terrible things in this life you will become dead to God in the next life. That is not it! We *start* this life dead to God and unless we do something to change that condition we will *stay* dead to God.

The Bible says:

> And you hath he quickened who were *dead in trespasses and sins*. Ephesians 2:1

The Bible says also:

> For *all* have sinned, and come short of the glory of God. Romans 3:23

'All'—the most inclusive word in the English language. It means you! It means a lot of other people as well but that is not of interest to you at this moment—it means you! You have sinned.

Who said so?

God said so in His Word!

What you have to do is to have a firm conviction within yourself that *you* are unworthy before God, that *you* have sinned. 'Hearing' God's Word means not only accepting it as being true but also applying it to *yourself*.

Sin is not something that happens to other people, it's something that has happened to you!

You will receive the gift of everlasting life only if you hear God's Word—there is no other way. It is futile saying 'Well I'm as good as those who go to church'; you may well be, or even better, but that is not the point at issue.

God judges you by His own standards and will not grant you everlasting life because you behave better than the person next door or better than the majority of people in the church down the road. Forget for a moment how good or bad the man or woman next door is, forget about that obscene rapist, forget about that dreadful murder you read about in the paper last week, forget even about the despicable and unspeakable who murdered millions in the concentration camps—their judgement is in the hands of God. You just worry about you—it's your eternal destiny we are talking about!

Do *not* compare yourself to other people and base your assessment of yourself on that—that is rather like saying of a burnt out car, 'Well at least it didn't go rusty.' God works by a very different standard—the standard of Jesus Christ.

Sometimes we fool ourselves

I'm sure you have heard the word 'rationalise'—the psychological meaning of the word is justifying yourself by either consciously or subconsciously telling yourself untruths—it stops you becoming hurt more than you can bear. We all do it at times but rationalising is something of which we should beware. Deceiving ourselves never changes the facts though it may make us feel better about them.

There's a better way than justifying yourself by rationalisation—it's letting God justify you through faith.

The Bible says:

> Being justified by *faith*, we have peace with God.
> Romans 5:1

Here's a classic case of rationalisation. Read the story of the rich young man who came to Jesus:

> And, behold, one came and said unto him, Good

> Master, what good thing shall I do, that I may have eternal life?
>
> And he [Jesus] said unto him, Why callest thou me good? There is none good but one, that is, God; but if thou wilt enter into life, keep the commandments.
>
> He said unto him, Which?
>
> Jesus said, Thou shalt do no murder, Thou shalt no commit adultery, Thou shalt not steal, Thou shalt not bear false witness, Honour thy father and thy mother; and, Thou shalt love thy neighbour as thyself.
>
> The young man saith unto him, All these things have I kept from my youth up. What lack I yet?
>
> Jesus said unto him, If thou wilt be perfect, go and sell what thou hast, and give to the poor, and thou shalt have treasure in heaven; and come and follow me.
>
> But when the young man heard that saying, he went away sorrowful; for he had great possessions.
>
> Matthew 19:16–22

We are all to a greater or lesser degree guilty of self-delusion. Some may call it hypocrisy but it is not that for we do not *intend* to present ourselves to others as something we are not—we actually subconsciously delude *ourselves* into believing that we are something we are not.

How incisive were the words of the Scottish poet Rabbie Burns when he wrote, 'I wish some power the gift would gi' us to see ourselves as others see us.'

Firstly, Jesus exposed that the rich young ruler had not received *the faith factor*. 'Why callest thou me good for there is none good but God.' Unlike Peter, who, as we have seen, had been 'given' his insight into the identity of Jesus from 'above', this young man spoke of Jesus as a good man. Jesus said in effect exactly what is said in another chapter in this book: 'Only God is good, if I am not God then why call me good?'

Here was a man who claimed to have kept the law of God from his youth but Jesus, very perceptively, put him to the acid test: 'Go sell all that thou hast and give to the poor.' But, we read, the rich man 'went away sorrowful for he had great possessions'.

Some have taken that to mean that you cannot be rich and be a Christian. That is not what it means at all! Solomon was rich and stayed in the will of God. Joseph of Arimathea, the rich man in whose tomb Jesus was buried, was a close follower of Jesus. Someone has pointed out too that if it had not been for a rich man we would not have the story of the good Samaritan. In the case of the rich young man what Jesus was doing was to put him to the test. You see we *all* have views of ourselves which are not accurate. The rich young man's view of himself was that he kept *all* the law; he probably believed that very sincerely. We *all* believe many things about ourselves which are not true.

One of the ten commandments was *thou shalt have no other gods before me*. The rich young man probably thought that he *did* only worship *one* God—how wrong he was! When Jesus gave him the choice between his riches on earth and riches in heaven the rich young man chose his earthly god. Joseph of Arimathea, on the other hand, put his possessions to the service of God, and the disciples on the Day of Pentecost shared their wordly wealth.

You wouldn't really say that you have never sinned—would you?

'*All* have sinned' does not just mean that sin is imputed to us. It means that we as individuals have sinned, each and every one of us.

Adam's sin was to disobey the Word of God which said 'the day that thou eatest thereof thou shalt surely die' and listen to the contrary voice which said 'thou shalt not surely die'. Can *you* say that you have always accepted the Word of God absolutely and applied it in your life? If you do say that, are you quite sure you are not making the same mistake the rich young man made?

Yes! You have sinned—will you accept it!

The Bible teaches that the wages of sin is death and you are in great peril—will you accept it?

Just as God said to Adam 'In the day that thou eatest thereof thou shalt surely die' (Genesis 2:17), so He has said to YOU and me in His Word:

> The wages of sin is death; but the gift of God is eternal life through Jesus Christ our Lord.
> Romans 6:23

> ...the soul that sinneth, it shall die.   Ezekiel 18:4

That seems to be the Catch 22 situation doesn't it? The fact that *all* have sinned and the fact that the wages of sin is death means we all, both by nature and by individual action, have incurred the Divine death penalty!

I have never yet met anyone who claimed that they

had never sinned in the whole of their life. I am sure *you* would make no such claim.

Drinking cyanide is not a matter of frequency or quantity

Now I am not suggesting that you are a bad person, on the contrary, you are probably a very good person, but goodness is not enough. I cannot emphasise too often or too strongly that no one ever received everlasting life on account of them being good. God does not judge us on the *amount* of sin we commit, only on the fact that we are sinners.

Sin is poison to God and it is poison to *your* soul! You don't have to drink cyanide *often* nor do you need to drink a *bucketful* of it for it to kill you. The effects of drinking cyanide have nothing to do with frequency or quantity, they only have to do with the potent nature of the stuff. Sin is potent, so potent that 'The soul that sinneth, it shall die.'

If sin is so potent what hope is there for us? If you drink poison the only hope is to find the antidote but you won't drink the antidote until you have a deep conviction that you are dying of the poison!

At this point you have to recognise that you have a *need* and depend upon the scriptural promise that '*whosoever* shall call upon the name of the Lord shall be saved.'

I was having dinner with a well known multi-millionaire, who also happened to be a devoted Catholic, and a rather famous actor who was an active Protestant Christian. The talk turned to religion and the actor said, 'Never mind, we'll get justice in the next life', to which my Catholic business friend replied, 'God forbid! I am looking for mercy *not* justice.' Which goes to show that no denomination has the sole option on truth. Mercy is my only hope and your only hope too!

The Bible teaches that we cannot rely upon good works to bring forgiveness of our sins—will you accept it?

I will repeat the quotation I have emphasised previously:

> For by grace are ye saved through faith; and that not of yourselves: it is the gift of God. *Not of works,* lest any man should boast.
> Ephesians 2:8–9

It stands to reason doesn't it that there's no point in tying apples on a plum tree hoping that by that means you change the nature of the plum tree. Whatever it is in the nature of the thing to be that it *will* be.

It is very sad to see well-meaning people trying, often without being consciously aware that they are doing so, to assuage their consciences and secure their eternal future by good work. Poison in your system does not go away when you laugh and you will not cure yourself of influenza by feeding a thousand hungry people or by giving your friend who has influenza an aspirin. You will not cure gangrene by spraying scent on it. You will not bring a dead relative back to life by either covering her face with rouge or donating a million pounds to charity in her name. You could not cure yourself of deafness by giving ten thousand pounds to a home for the deaf nor of blindness by being ever so kind to the blind.

To think that you can change your eternal status by

being a 'good sort' or doing good works is to misunderstand the nature of sin and how it affects your spiritual life. Sin is *not* the absence of good works, sin is a part of human nature, a malady upon human nature that cannot be put to rights by doing something for someone else.

Though we may cover the rough wood of human nature with a veneer of civilisation, from time to time the veneer becomes scratched and we see real, unregenerate man underneath and we are inclined to despair of mankind getting any better or even surviving.

An adder is venomous because it *is* an adder, it is not an adder because it is venomous. Paint an adder a different colour and it will still be an adder; there is nothing you can do to change the nature of the thing, that is the way it is born.

When Jesus said 'Ye must be born again' He was saying that an act of miraculous, supernatural re-creation must take place in a person's life before their nature is changed.

As the Apostle Paul said:

> If any man be in Christ, he is a new creation; old things have passed away; behold *all* things have become new. 2 Corinthians 5:17

There is nothing you can do to work *for* salvation or to purchase salvation, there is nothing you can do to earn salvation except to accept the sacrifice already made for you at Calvary.

The ancient Israelites were instructed to build their altars thus:

> If thou wilt make me an altar of stone, thou shalt not built it of hewn stone; for if thou lift up thy tool

upon it, thou hast polluted it. Neither shalt thou go up by steps unto my altar, that thy nakedness be not discovered thereon. Exodus 20:25–26

The altar was, of course, the place of forgiveness where the sacrifice for sin was made. That altar was not to be made of hewn stone—no effort was to go into building it! It foreshadowed the scripture 'not of works lest any man should boast'. Yet people still think that they can build an altar of good works and that God will recognise it!

'Thou shalt make no steps to my altar' refers to the fact that there is no preparation necessary for a person to come to Christ. You cannot *prepare* yourself for the day you come and accept the sacrifice of Jesus and say *He died for me*. It matters not how vile your life may have been or how good, for that matter; there is no preparation you can make—you have to come just as you are.

Throughout the ages hymnwriters and churches of all denominations have recognised our helplessness when we come to Christ:

> Just as I am, without one plea,
> But that Thy blood was shed for me,
> And that Thou bidst me come to Thee,
> O Lamb of God, I come.

> Just as I am, and waiting not,
> To rid my soul of one dark blot,
> To Thee, whose blood can cleanse each spot,
> O Lamb of God, I come.

> Just as I am—though tossed about
> With many a conflict, many a doubt,

Fightings and fears within, without,
O Lamb of God, I come.

Just as I am, Thou wilt receive,
Wilt welcome, pardon, cleanse, relieve;
Because Thy promise I believe,
O Lamb of God, I come.

That hymn contains the very substance of what this book is about.

The Bible teaches that you cannot rely on church membership for your salvation—will you accept it?

The church, by which I mean the congregation of Christians who worship together, *united* in one faith and *separated* by their denominational names, is a very important institution.

It is a command of God, and remember, sin is disobedience to the command of God, that every Christian should belong to a local church. The Apostle Paul wrote:

> Let us hold fast the profession of our faith without wavering (for he is faithful that promised); and let us consider one another to provoke unto love and to good works: *not forsaking the assembling of ourselves together,* as the manner of some is, but exhorting one another, and so much the more, as ye see the day approaching.   Hebrews 10:23–25

Truth carried to extremes will always result in error and that is exactly what has happened regarding church membership. There *have* been times in the history of the Christian church when certain sections of the church have taught, or implied, that to belong to this or that religious organisation is all that is necessary to ensure salvation.

On the other hand there have been those who have altogether denigrated church membership and taught that there is really no need to belong to a local church. They often use phrases such as 'As long as you belong to the Lord you can worship Him in your own home or in the garden, you don't need to go to church.' It is interesting to ask those who argue like that, 'How many other of God's commandments can you break and still claim to be a Christian?'

Both views are overstatements of certain truths. The Bible requires *all* believers to be church members but plainly teaches that church membership in itself will not bring about salvation.

Stated plainly the fact is that you *should* be a church member because you are a Christian, you are *not* a Christian because you are a church member.

Just as a child needs the family so the Christian needs the church. In the best of local churches the new Christian will find fellowship, teaching, and support in a sometimes hostile world. Though you *can* be a Christian without going to church you will not develop your spirituality to the extent you would if you attended a spiritual local church.

The Bible teaches that no one is a Christian by reason of their nationality—will you accept it?

It has been thought by some, and taught by a few, that if you were born in a Christian country you are, unless you opt out, a Christian. Strictly speaking, of course, there is no such thing as a 'Christian country', though I think we all know what is meant by that term.

A PROMISE FROM GOD TO YOU

Even descendants of Abraham, Isaac and Jacob, though members of God's chosen people, did not automatically inherit everlasting life. Speaking to the Pharisees and the Sadducees, members of the 'chosen race', Israel, Jesus said:

> O generation of vipers, who hath warned you to flee from the wrath to come? Matthew 3:7

They were members of the chosen race but they were not children of God.

In another scripture Jesus is recorded as saying:

> Ye are of your father the devil, and the lusts of your father ye will do. John 8:44

It was to Nicodemus, an Israelite of the house of Judah, that Jesus said:

> Unless a man be *born again,* he cannot see the kingdom of God. John 3:3–5

The Bible says:

> For by one Spirit are we all baptized into one body, whether we be Jews or Gentiles, whether we be bond or free; and have all been made to drink into one Spirit. 1 Corinthians 12:13

You may pride yourself on the fact that you live in a nation that has done more than any other to propagate the gospel and you would be rightly proud of that. You may pride yourself on being born into a nation which still, despite declining standards in some areas of our national life and what we read in the press, seeks officially to extol Christian virtues. Perhaps you have reflected on the amount of food your nation sends to the starving people of the world and felt a sense of gratification that you are a part of it.

You are right to be proud of all that, you are right to love your country and be patriotic but you must not depend upon that for *your* salvation.

Whatever the official religion of the country in which you were born and in which you live, whether that be voodoo or Christianity, you can only come to possess eternal life according to Jesus' promise when *you* receive *the faith factor* and *you* come into a personal relationship with Him in the way He has ordained.

God does not dispense salvation to groups of people, whether they be national groups or religious groups. God will only deal with individuals on a one to one basis through Christ.

The Bible teaches that you cannot depend upon the sacraments for salvation — will you accept that?

I want to be very careful here because the sacraments are very important to the Christian faith and I do not want to detract at all from their importance. It is a commandment of the Lord Jesus Christ Himself that we should partake of the sacraments.

The sacraments are an outward declaration of an inward work. Baptism does not save you — it is there as a sacrament for those who have already accepted Christ as their personal Saviour, a testimony to the fact that they have died to the old life and are resurrected to new life.

The bread and wine, called the Lord's Supper by some and Holy Communion by others, does not save you. In fact the Bible is very strict about the partaking of the emblems. It says:

> For I have received of the Lord that which also I delivered unto you, that the Lord Jesus, the same night in which he was betrayed, took bread; and when he had given thanks, he broke it, and said, Take, eat; this is my body which is broken for you: this do in remembrance of me.
> After the same manner also he took the cup, when he had supped, saying, This cup is the new testament in my blood: this do ye, as often as ye drink it, in remembrance of me.
> For as often as ye eat this bread, and drink this cup, ye do show the Lord's death till he come. Wherefore, whosoever shall eat this bread, and drink this cup of the Lord unworthily, shall be guilty of the body and blood of the Lord.
>
> 1 Corinthians 11:23–27

No one has any right to partake of the sacraments until *after* they have come to know Christ as their personal Saviour.

The Bible teaches that without the shedding of blood there is no remission of sin—will you accept it?

Years ago when we all went to Sunday school we were so instructed in the basic ideas of the Christian faith that we were used to religious terminology. Now we are less used to it. Time was when a preacher could ask 'Are you washed in the blood of the Lamb' and even the unconverted would know what he meant and would either reply 'yes' or 'no'. These days most people would smile and ask, 'Whatever are you talking about?'

The Bible says:

> Without the shedding of blood there is no remission. Hebrews 9:22

You will remember me saying of the Bible earlier on in this book that 'The Old is in the New revealed and the New is in the Old concealed.'

Though the Bible consists of sixty-six separate books, written over a period of thousands of years, and though many of the writers never met, it is the most consistent book in the world.

Let's look at that statement, 'Without the shedding of blood there is no remission (of sins)', for a moment. The theme is developed but never altered from the first chapter of Genesis to the last chapter of Revelation.

Substitutional death in Genesis

The subject is so important that it is first introduced in the Garden of Eden immediately after the fall of Adam:

> For Adam also and for his wife did the Lord God make coats of skins, and clothed them.
> Genesis 3:21

It is surprising how many people believe that Adam and Eve wore fig leaves! When you think of it, it is the most sensible kind of garment for God to have chosen. Think how easy it would have been to clothe them in clothes woven from the wool of a lamb or grass. Why did God not do that?

The answer is, because He was providing us with a 'word picture' showing us that without the shedding of blood there is no remission of sins.

Adam and Eve, looking at the animal, the skin of which had been used to cover their nakedness, would be able to say *'He died for me.'*

Cain and Abel

Turn to the story of Cain and Abel:

> And Adam knew Eve his wife; and she conceived, and bore Cain, and said, I have gotten a man from the Lord.
>
> And she again bore his brother Abel. And Abel was a keeper of sheep, but Cain was a tiller of the ground. And in the process of time it came to pass, that Cain brought of the fruit of the ground an offering unto the Lord.
>
> And Abel, he also brought of the firstlings of his flock and of the fat thereof. And the Lord had respect unto Abel and to his offering.
>
> But to Cain and to his offering he had no respect. Genesis 4:1–5

Both were sincere, both believed in God, both worshipped God, and both brought sacrifices. The sacrifice brought by Cain was rejected. Arguably Cain worked harder to produce the 'fruit of the ground' than Abel did in tending his flock but God rejected the bloodless sacrifice because *without the shedding of blood there is no remission of sins*.

The sin of Cain was *not* in the fact that he brought the 'fruit of the ground' to God as an act of worship; the sin was that he depended on a bloodless sacrifice for his salvation. Notice carefully the difference between bringing a thank offering to God and relying on that offering for salvation.

You can imagine Abel, whose sacrifice was accepted, looking at the sacrificial lamb and saying *'He died for me.'*

But there is a further and perhaps deeper point to be made here. How did Abel *know* what was the correct sacrifice to bring—nobody had told him! The answer is that he had *the faith factor* which Cain did not have and which we find recorded in Hebrews:

> By *faith* Abel offered unto God a more excellent sacrifice than Cain, by which he obtained witness that he was righteous. Hebrews 11:4

Abraham and Isaac

Come forward with me to the days of Abraham and read:

> And it came to pass after these things, that God did test Abraham, and said unto him, Abraham: and he said, Behold, here I am. And he said, Take now thy son, thine only son Isaac, whom thou lovest, and get thee into the land of Moriah; and offer him there for a burnt offering upon one of the mountains which I will tell thee of.
>
> And Abraham rose up early in the morning, and saddled his ass, and took two of his young men with him, and Isaac his son, and cut the wood for the burnt offering, and rose up, and went unto the place of which God had told him. Then on the third

A PROMISE FROM GOD TO YOU

day Abraham lifted up his eyes, and saw the place afar off.

And Abraham said unto his young men, Abide ye here with the ass; and I and the lad will go yonder and worship, and come again to you. And Abraham took the wood of the burnt offering, and laid it upon Isaac his son; and he took the fire in his hand, and a knife; and they were both of them together.

And Isaac spoke unto Abraham his father, and said...Behold the fire and the wood; but where is the lamb for the burnt offering?

And Abraham said, My son, God will provide himself a lamb for a burnt offering: so they went both of them together.

And they came to the place which God had told him of; and Abraham built an altar there, and laid the wood in order, and bound Isaac his son, and laid him on the altar upon the wood. And Abraham stretched forth his hand, and took the knife to slay his son.

And the angel of the Lord called unto him out of heaven, and said, Abraham, Abraham; and he said, Here am I.

And he said, Lay not thy hand upon the lad, neither do thou anything unto him; for now I know that thou fearest God, seeing thou hast not withheld thy son, thine only son from me.

And Abraham lifted up his eyes, and looked, and, behold, behind him a ram caught in a thicket by his horns: and Abraham went and took the ram, and offered him up for a burnt offering in the stead of his son.   Genesis 22:1–13

We can imagine Isaac stepping from the altar, looking at the body of the ram and saying *'He died for me.'*

The concept of substitutional death, vicarious sacrifice, or *'He died for me'*, was extended at the Passover. A nation was now involved.

The Passover

Israel was in Egypt suffering terrible persecution. Every attempt by Moses to have Pharaoh let his people go had ended in failure. It was indicated to Moses that judgement would come upon Egypt smiting all the firstborn in the land. There was to be one way of escape:

> Then Moses called for all the elders of Israel, and said unto them, Draw out and take you a lamb according to your families, and kill the passover. And ye shall take a bunch of hyssop, and dip it in the blood that is in the basin, and strike the lintel and two side posts with the blood that is in the basin; and none of you shall go out at the door of his house until the morning.
> For the Lord will pass through to smite the Egyptians; and when he seeth the blood upon the lintel, and on the two side posts, the Lord will pass over the door, and will not permit the destroyer to come into your houses to smite you. Exodus 12:21–23

One can visualise how, when the Israelites emerged into the grey light of morning and saw the carnage around them, they would think of the lamb they had slain and say *'He died for me.'*

Some 1,600 years later Paul was to draw attention to this symbolic happening:

A PROMISE FROM GOD TO YOU

> For even Christ, our *passover,* is slain for us.
> 1 Corinthians 5:7

The Passover was the ultimate in 'word pictures' of the death of Jesus on Calvary.

The Lamb slain for the world

Now read of the moment when John the Baptist said of Jesus:

> The next day John seeth Jesus coming unto him, and saith, Behold the Lamb of God, who taketh away the sin of the world. John 1:29

You will see the development of the theme *'He died for me'* throughout the Bible. Of course I have mentioned but a few of the thousands of 'word pictures' which are in the Old Testament and which relate to the coming of Jesus. The trappings and ritual of the Tabernacle in the Wilderness are alive with 'word pictures' of the coming Jesus. The Temple too spoke of Jesus.

As you progress in the Christian faith you will find the relationship between Jesus and the Old Testament fascinating but for the moment let me just stick to this one phrase *'He died for me.'*

The Bible teaches that each individual has to accept Jesus Christ as his own personal sacrifice—will you accept that?

It is important to recognise that, though the lamb died and was the sacrifice for sin, the individual part of the transaction was that it only became efficacious when the individual *accepted the sacrifice as being for him.*

The application of the blood by the Israelites to the lintels of their houses is typical of the necessity for each and every one of us to recognise the death of Christ upon Calvary as being for each of us as individuals.

There is an essential step which is beyond God's provision for you—it is *your* personal acceptance of that provision.

Adam would not have been clothed *had he not put the clothes on,* despite the fact the provision had been made for him.

Abel would not have found favour with God if he had *allowed someone else* to take the lamb for him. It had to be a personal thing between him and God.

Isaac would not have been saved if Abraham had left the ram in the thicket; the provision was made by God but it had to be *personally appropriated and accepted.*

The firstborn of the Israelites would have died along with the Egyptians had *they not used the blood* on the lintels of their houses; they had the *revelation,* they had the *provision* but neither worked for them until they accepted the revelation and the provision in a *personal way.*

You may have the revelation *the faith factor*, and God has certainly made *the provision* for your salvation, but neither will work for you unless you personally appropriate the provision God has made.

Jesus died for the sins of the *world* but, as with the other sacrificial lambs we have mentioned, His shed blood will not work *for you* unless *you* accept Him as *your own personal blood sacrifice and saviour.*

If you reject the sacrifice of Jesus there is no other way that you can be cleansed of your sins.

As the Bible says:

> Christ being come an high priest of good things to come, by a greater and more perfect tabernacle, not made with hands, that is to say, not of this building; neither by the blood of goats and calves, but by his own blood he entered in once into the holy place, *having obtained eternal redemption for us*.
>
> For if the blood of bulls and of goats, and the ashes of an heifer sprinkling the unclean, sanctifieth to the purifying of the flesh, how much more shall the blood of Christ, who through the eternal Spirit offered himself without spot to God, purge your conscience from dead works to serve the living God?
> Hebrews 9:11–14

Have you accepted all that? Then in the next chapter we will discuss the word 'believeth' and its meaning in Jesus' promise 'He that heareth my word and *believeth* on him that sent me, hath everlasting life and shall not come into condemnation but is passed from death unto life.'

8 *What Jesus meant by believing*

JUST AS THE WORD 'hearing' does not always mean merely hearing the sound of someone's voice so the word 'believing' has another meaning than the superficial one.

Some use the words 'faith' and 'believe' interchangeably—they should not be used in that way. As we have seen faith is not belief, it is the God-given *ability* to believe.

Jesus said, 'He that heareth my word and *believeth* on him that sent me, hath everlasting life' (John 5:24).

If you have asked, sought and knocked you will now have faith or, in other words, *the ability to believe*. I know you will because Jesus promised that *everyone* who asked would receive, *everyone* who sought would find and *everyone* who knocked would have the door opened unto them.

Now let us look at this phrase 'and believeth on him that sent me'.

The word 'believe' is used very loosely by many people. 'Will Tom be in work today?' 'I believe so.' It means the person is not quite sure. That is, of course, *not* the meaning of the word 'believeth' when used by Jesus in the above quotation.

For example, the phrase 'I believe in elephants' does not say anything about your relationship with elephants. It says only that you believe that an animal called an elephant exists.

You may 'believe' in elephants and hate them, you may 'believe' in elephants and be indifferent to them or you may 'believe' in elephants and love them. Every hunter who hunts elephants, kills them and disposes of their carcass for profit believes in elephants.

Belief is not just giving intellectual assent

So when Jesus said '...and believeth on him that sent me' He was not speaking of an intellectual assent to the existence of God. As with the elephant, the fact that you believe in God does not say anything about your relationship with God. You may 'believe' in Him and hate Him, you may 'believe' in Him and be indifferent to Him or you may 'believe' in Him and love Him.

The Apostle James wrote:

> Thou believest that there is one God; thou doest well: the devils also believe, and tremble.
> James 2:19

From that we see that the devils have no superficial belief such as we find among people who profess to believe in a 'one above'. Their belief in God is so profound that they 'tremble'. Few people actually tremble before God these days which just goes to show that their belief in God is not really as profound as the devils' belief in God.

Obviously the kind of belief which leaves people unchanged in their attitude to God is not what Jesus meant!

The word translated 'believeth' is, in the original language, *pisteuo*, and means to trust, to rely on, *to become one with* and to adhere to.

Do you believe?

Let me take you to a great international airport. You want to fly to New York and there is a plane on the runway which is scheduled to fly to New York.

You have *heard* that aeroplanes are *capable* of taking people to New York haven't you?

'Yes, of course.'

Do you *believe* that the New York flight exists?

'Yes.'

Then get on it and it will take you where you want to go!

'No.'

Let me ask you: Though you know about aeroplanes and believe that they can take you to your destination do you think they will perform their function for *you* if you don't get on board?

You feel ill and the doctor says, 'I'll give you an antibiotic, that will put you right.'

You have heard of antibiotics haven't you?

'Yes.'

Do you *believe* that this antibiotic *will* cure you?

'Yes.'

So you take the antibiotic tablets home and leave them in the bottle. Do you think they will cure *you?*

No aeroplane will get you from here to there unless *you* get on it. No medicine will cure *your* ills unless you take it. No salvation will save *you* unless you trust it for your salvation.

Believing is not *giving mental* assent to the existence of God, it is *trusting* God and accepting His Word.

Hearing—believing—taking!

I have dedicated this book to my father and mother who both knew Christ and kept the faith until they were called into the presence of the Lord. They were brought to Christ through the ministry of that great revivalist/preacher and my good friend the late Principal George Jeffreys. I would like to think that this book is also something of a thanksgiving for his mighty ministry. He used to sum up our quotation from John 5:24 in this way:

HEARING!
BELIEVING!
TAKING!

The auditorium would be thronged with people and thousands of voices would blend in the haunting refrain:

> Just as I am without one plea,
> Save that Thy blood was shed for me,
> And that Thou bidst me come to Thee,
> Oh, Lamb of God—I come.
>
> Just as I am, Thy love unknown,
> Has broken every barrier down,
> Now to be Thine, yea Thine alone,
> Oh Lamb of God—I come.

With the singing going on in the background he used to say that if his hearers believed God and if they trusted God they would take God at His Word. He would then quote the promise, *'whosoever shall call upon the name of the Lord shall be saved.'*

Then he would give two illustrations of people who called upon the name of the Lord and were saved. The first was the publican we find mentioned in Luke 18:13 who cried, 'Lord be merciful to me a sinner', and the second the dying thief mentioned in Luke 23:42 who cried, 'Lord, remember me when thou comest into thy kingdom.'

He would make the point that a long prayer was unnecessary, all that was needed was a short *call* from the heart. He would conclude with this little bit of supposed dialogue between himself and an imaginary member of his congregation:

'Jesus said call—did you call?'

'Yes, Mr Jeffreys I did.'

'What are you now?'

'Saved!'

'Who told you you are saved?'

'God told me in His Word that I am saved.'

It was simple but I have seen the most learned people brought to Christ in that way.

I think you would do well to make that simple *call* today.

The sincere call from the heart

There is sometimes a feeling among us, yes even among we who have been Christians for a long time, that somehow our prayers are not long enough, not grand enough and not theological enough. When such fears assail us we should read the instructions Jesus gave concerning prayer:

> And when thou prayest, thou shalt not be as the hypocrites are; for they love to pray standing in the synagogues and in the corners of the streets, that they may be seen by men. Verily I say unto you, They have their reward.
>
> But thou, when thou prayest, enter into thy room and shut thy door, pray to thy Father who is in secret; and thy Father, who seeth in secret, shall reward thee openly.
>
> But when ye pray, use not vain repetitions, as the pagans do; for they think they shall be heard for their much speaking.
>
> Be not ye, therefore, like unto them; for your Father knoweth what things ye have need of, before ye ask him. Matthew 6:5–8

The fact is that a few sincere words in the quietness of your bedroom or anywhere else for that matter are as effective with God as any long poetic exhibition. Grand language does not impress God—He's heard it all before and been quite unimpressed by the sincerity of some who have used it.

Stick to the simple prayer 'Lord be merciful to me a sinner'—it works!

So that is what the word 'believeth', as used by Jesus, really means:

Believing does not mean giving mental assent to a code of conduct; it means to accept the Word of God in its entirety, both the written word (the Bible) and the Living Word (the Lord Jesus Christ).

Believing means not only to accept God's Word but also to apply it to yourself.

Believing means to rely upon Jesus and let Him take control of your life.

Believing means surrendering your life to Jesus Christ and the absorption of His very nature into your being so that you are no longer your own person but *His*.

9 *Born into the new dimension*

THE BIBLE TELLS of two worlds—one is the world of the flesh and the other the world of the spirit.

To enter this physical world we have to be born into it—that is evident to all of us because we have all undergone that experience. What is not evident to all of us is that if we wish to enter into the world of the Spirit, the new dimension, we have to be born into it—that is what is meant by being born again.

I quote the following Bible passage at length because the new birth is one of the most important concepts of the scriptures:

> There was a man of the Pharisees, named Nicodemus, a ruler of the Jews;
>
> The same came to Jesus by night, and said unto him, Rabbi, we know that thou art a teacher come from God; for no man can do the miracles that thou doest, except God be with him.

> Jesus answered and said unto him, Verily, verily, I say unto thee, Except a man be born again, he cannot *see* the kingdom of God.
>
> Nicodemus saith unto him, How can a man be born when he is old? Can he enter a second time into his mother's womb, and be born?
>
> Jesus answered, Verily, verily, I say unto thee, Except a man be born of water and of the Spirit, he cannot *enter* into the kingdom of God.
>
> That which is born of the flesh is flesh; and that which is born of the Spirit is spirit.   John 3:1–6

The man to whom Jesus addressed His remark was a Pharisee and a teacher in Israel. He knew the Scriptures and he adhered to the true faith of his time. He believed Jesus to be a teacher sent from God, a belief based upon the evidence of the miracles Jesus performed. This man was no critic of Jesus, he was obviously *an admirer* of Jesus and His works.

Jesus' reply would at first seem to be out of context and disjointed: 'Jesus answered, and said unto him, Verily, verily, I say unto thee, Except a man be born again, he cannot *see* the kingdom of God.'

It is not until we realise that to recognise as a 'teacher sent from God' and to consider Him to be a Rabbi is not enough that we realise that Jesus' reply is not out of context. Here was a man, doubtless a good living man, a man with a considerable knowledge of theology, a man who believed that Jesus was sent from God, a man who accepted the miracles that Jesus did as being the works of God. 'No,' said Jesus, 'you've got it all wrong! You do not recognise who I am because you *cannot see into my world*. You've got a good knowledge of *this* physical world but no appreciation of the world of the Spirit.

Unless a man be born again he cannot *see* the kingdom of God.'

Nicodemus replied, 'How can a man be born when he is old? Can he enter a second time into his mother's womb, and be born?' (John 3:4).

He proved the point Jesus was making! Though he was able to recognise Jesus as a man sent from God and that the works of Jesus were of God, this man could not cross the divide between the two dimensions, that of the physical and that of the spiritual. The mind of Nicodemus could not see beyond the physical. Unlike the dying thief and Peter, lesser intellectuals and lesser theologians, he could not recognise in Jesus *the Lord of glory*.

Jesus said, 'That which is born of the flesh is flesh; and that which is born of the Spirit is spirit.'

The new birth is no mere reformation of character

Some would have it that the new birth spoken of by Jesus is simply a new beginning—it is much more than that!

There are, of course, those who consider the Christian faith to be a philosophy, a code of conduct and it is to be expected that to those holding that view the new birth would signify the time when a person changed from his old philosophy to the new philosophy and from the old code of conduct to the new code of conduct.

That does not take into account what really happens to a person when they are born again. The new birth is not simply a change of heart or a change of conduct—it is the *re-creation* of a person.

> Behold, what manner of love the Father hath bestowed upon us, *that we should be called the sons*

> *of God;* therefore the world knoweth us not, because it knew him not.
>
> Beloved, now are we the sons of God, and it doth not yet appear what we shall be: but we know that, when he shall appear, we shall be like him; for we shall see him as he is. 1 John 3:1–2

Born-again Christians are not merely their old selves tidied up and dusted down, they are quite literally new creations in Christ Jesus, being, as the Bible tells us, 'Born again, not of corruptible but incorruptible, by the word of the Lord' (1 Peter 1:23). That phrase 'by the word of the Lord' takes us back to Genesis when physical man was first brought into being by the word of the Lord.

Just as you did not exist in this physical world before your natural conception so you will not exist in the spiritual world until you are born again into that world.

The new birth is a new beginning

Now I'm not contradicting myself! I said that the new birth was not *only* a new beginning, not that it was *not* a new beginning.

When you were born the first time, into the world of flesh, you entered into a world in which you had previously not existed, a world of which you had no experience or perception—you had a new beginning. No blame could be attached to you because you had never committed any act either good or bad. You had no previous record of any kind!

That is precisely the position in which a person finds himself when he becomes born again. Whatever happened prior to the new birth *becomes non-existent* because it happened prior to that birth.

'Don't blame me I wasn't born then!'

I once listened to a grand sermon preached by a preacher from the deep south of America and it went something like this: 'Sometimes that old devil comes along and tells me all the things I did before I was saved. "Joe you robbed people's houses and you almost killed a man. You went to prison for dishonest dealing and for assault." I say to the old devil, "No you wrong! I didn't do none of those things 'cos I wasn't even born then." That's what I always tell the old devil, "Don't you go accusing Joe of doing things before he was born".'

The fact is that nothing you have done before the day you are born again counts before God. You may have lied, you may have cheated, you may have done all kinds of harm to other people, you may have raped and even murdered—the day you are born again the whole lot is wiped out! Not only does God not condemn you for it, He forgives you for it and *forgets all about it*. The Bible says:

> I will forgive their iniquity, and I will remember their sin no more. Jeremiah 31:34

In the Psalms the Bible says:

> He hath not dealt with us after our sins, nor rewarded us accordingly to our iniquities. For as the heaven is high above the earth, so great is his mercy toward them that fear him. *As far as the east*

> *is from the west, so far hath he removed our transgressions from us.* Psalm 103:10–12

We often hear people say 'I forgive but I don't forget'—I have never really known what they mean by that! Certainly it is not an attitude which emanates from the Spirit of Christ. God forgives *and* forgets and God's people should both forgive and forget.

I am typing this on a computer. Everything I write is being recorded on a disk. There is an instruction I can give the computer which will completely erase everything on the disk on which I am working. That's what God does when you become born again: He presses a button which erases all record of you before you were born again—to Him your past becomes non-existent.

In the Scriptures God had a wonderful way of demonstrating this new beginning—He changed the name of the people He called to do His service. Abram's was changed to Abraham, Jacob's name was changed to Israel, Simon's name was changed to Peter and Saul's name was changed to Paul. Yes the break with the past is that complete—a true *new birth*.

The new birth—the ultimate mystical experience

Though it is the business of every Christian to feed the hungry, tend the sick and minister to those in need, the Christian faith should not be propagated or thought of as a welfare organisation.

The Christian's battle is of a much higher and much more mystical kind.

Because the miraculous aspect of Christianity has not been stressed and because Christianity has been reduced by some to nothing more than a philosophy, a way of life, many have turned to occult practices in search of personal power.

The fact is that there is no initiation ceremony known to the occult which can give an individual nearly as much personal power as the *new birth* experience.

Each and every man and woman who is filled with the Spirit of Christ is more powerful spiritually than any black-magician.

The Apostle Paul makes it abundantly plain that the Christian life is not merely a battle against poverty and hunger, not merely a high minded philosophy but a battle against supernatural forces that exist in the spirit world (Ephesians 6:11–12).

In Luke we read that Jesus sent seventy believers out to preach the gospel and we read:

> And the seventy returned again with joy, saying, Lord, even the devils are subject unto us through thy name.　　　　　　　　　　　　Luke 10:17

By all means feed the hungry, by all means look after the homeless and by all means love the sheer beauty of the Scriptures but never forget *the power of the name of Jesus*. All the ills of mankind are but fruits of that battle against all principalities and powers spoken of by the Apostle Paul. Satanic power is very real and so is the power of the name of Jesus!

We are warned by the Apostle Paul that one of the signs of the last days and the imminent return of Jesus Christ will be people 'Having a form of godliness but denying the power of it; from such turn away' (2 Timothy 3:5).

One only has to read the experiences of people like the Revd Christopher Neil-Smith, vicar of St Saviour's

Church, Hampstead, in North London, England, to appreciate the full extent of the truth of which Paul was writing and to recognise the power in Christ a Christian has over the forces of evil. The Revd Neil-Smith has been described as Britain's leading exorcist.

Though written, not from a Christian but from a secular point of view, a reading of *The Real Exorcists*, written by Leslie Watkins and published by Methuen, is well worth while. The author is a professional writer who had investigated the phenomenon known as devil or demon possession. He not only deals with devil possession from a theoretical point of view but eschews hearsay and tells of his experiences at actual exorcism sessions.

Anyone who reads Mr Watkin's book will be left in no doubt that terrible supernatural evil influences abound in the real world and that supreme spiritual power resides in the true Christian faith.

Just as a black-magician can become devil possessed so the Christian becomes God possessed.

When we are born again we become partakers of Divine life

We have seen that the word 'believe' as used by Jesus means 'to trust', 'to adhere to' and 'to become one with' God.

Accepting Christ is much more than merely accepting a code of conduct or a set of beliefs—it initiates a miraculous happening. The Spirit of God Himself takes up residence in you, not figuratively speaking but quite literally. The Apostle Paul wrote:

> I am crucified with Christ: nevertheless I live; yet not I, but *Christ liveth in me*.   Galatians 2:20

I am going to quote extensively from the Bible now because some of the things it tells us happen when a person believes in Christ are so profound as to need the authority of God's Word itself to confirm that the statements are valid.

When we are born again the Spirit of God comes to dwell within us

> If the Spirit of him that raised up Jesus from the dead dwell in you, he that raised up Christ from the dead shall also quicken your mortal bodies by his Spirit.
> Romans 8:11

That is an exciting thought, isn't it? The very same Spirit that entered the tomb of Jesus on that resurrection day, rolled the stone away and brought forth the resurrected Christ, enters OUR mortal bodies when we become born again.

When we are born again we become members of the body of Christ

When we accept Christ a supernatural process takes place—we become members of the body of Christ. God works a miracle in us. The Apostle Paul wrote:

> For by one Spirit are we all baptized into one body, whether we be Jews or Gentiles, whether we be bond or free; and have all been made to drink into one Spirit.
> 1 Corinthians 12:13

When we are born again we become partakers of Divine nature

A very unusual incident happened during the ministry of Jesus and Jesus spoke some very unusual words. Perhaps I have not been in the right place at the right time but I cannot remember ever having heard a sermon preached on these words. Yet they show how completely the absorption of Jesus into the believer and the believer into Jesus is. To me this scripture is at the very centre of the total identification of the believer with his Lord.

> Then Jesus said unto them, Verily, verily, I say unto you, except ye eat the flesh of the Son of man, and drink his blood, there is no life in you. He who eateth my flesh, and drinketh my blood, hath eternal life; and I will raise him up at the last day. For my flesh is food indeed, and my blood is drink indeed. He that eateth my flesh, and drinketh my blood, dwelleth in me and I in him...Many, therefore, of his disciples, when they heard this, said this is a hard saying...From that time many of his disciples went back, and walked no more with him.
> John 6: parts of verses 53–66

Needless to say, Jesus was not advocating cannibalism. He was making a point which is obscured when one thinks of Him as merely a great teacher and of Christianity as a profound philosophy.

What happens to food when we eat? We digest it and having done so it becomes an inseparable part of us. It is not merely attached to us—it is absorbed into our very being. That is the relationship a born-again Christian has with God. He or she becomes absorbed into God and God into him.

By which are given unto us exceedingly great and precious promises, that by these ye might be *partakers of the divine nature*... 2 Peter 1:4

When we are born again we receive power to become the sons of God

Much confusion has been caused by some describing *all* human beings as being sons of God. Strictly speaking God is *not* the Father of all men. He *is* the creator of all men but that is quite a different matter.

When Jesus said to the Pharisees:

> If God were your Father, ye would love me; for I proceeded forth and came from God; neither came I of myself, but he sent me... Ye are of your father the devil, and the lusts of your father ye will do.
> John 8:42,44

The Bible says:

> He came unto his own, and his own received him not. But as many received him, to them gave he power to *become* the sons of God, even to them that believe on his name: who were born, not of blood, nor of the will of the flesh, *nor of the will of man,* but of God. John 1:11–13

When it is said 'To as many as received him to them gave he power to *become* the sons of God' it is evident that He did not regard everyone as being sons of God for how can one *become* something that one already is? You have to have a special power to become a son, and by that I also mean daughter, of God and that power is a power He gave to 'as many as received Him'. You can only become a son by birth—in this case through the new birth.

When we are born again we become joint heirs with Christ

> But when the fulness of the time had come, God sent forth his Son, made of a woman, made under the law, to redeem them that were under the law, that we might receive the adoption of sons. And *because we are sons,* God hath sent forth the Spirit of his son into our hearts, crying, Father. Wherefore thou art no more a servant, but a son; and if a son, then an heir of God through Christ.
> Galatians 4:4–7

Think for a moment of that phrase 'an heir of God'. Sometimes we read the Bible and fail to realise the depth of meaning in the language used. The dictionary defines the word 'heir' like this: 'A person receiving or entitled to receive property or rank as the legal representative of the owner... an heir by right of blood... a direct descendant.'

> Blessed be the God and Father of our Lord Jesus Christ, who, according to his abundant mercy, hath begotten us again unto a living hope by the resurrection of Jesus Christ from the dead, to an *inheritance* incorruptible, and undefiled, and that fadeth not away, reserved in heaven for you, who are kept by the power of God through faith unto salvation ready to be revealed in the last time. 1 Peter 1:3–5

A new nature

'Doesn't he look like his father!' or 'Doesn't she look like her mother!' are exclamations we often hear about newborn babies. Of course as the child grows the likeness may either increase or decrease as genetic inheritance is modified by environment. We know that both physical and psychological characteristics are inherited from our parents and much, much more. There are so many ways in which we are 'like' our parents because we are their children.

The *second birth* ensures that we inherit the characteristics of one who has become the partaker of Divine nature.

> His divine power hath given unto us all things that pertain unto life and godliness, through the knowledge of him that hath called us to glory and virtue.
> By which are given unto us exceedingly great and precious promises, that by these *ye may be partakers of divine nature,* having escaped the corruption that is in the world through lust.
>
> 2 Peter 1:3–4

Now don't just read on—meditate for a while on that absolutely startling statement. We human beings, through the new birth, actually become partakers of the very nature and essence of God!

By natural birth all of us are sons of Adam—people without the ability to perceive that other world which is the domain of God. To change family we have to accept that 'To as many as believed in him to them gave he power to become the sons of God.' Becoming a son of God does not happen by your first birth nor by chance—

it is something that happens by Divine power through the second birth. 'Ye MUST,' said Jesus, 'be born again.'

10 *Generation—Degeneration—Regeneration*

THE STORY OF HUMANKIND can be summed up in three words—generation, degeneration and regeneration. That is what this chapter is about, but first let us recapitulate on the things we have read so far.

We have seen that God is spirit and cannot be discerned by the unaided human intellect or senses. 'No man has seen God at any time' (1 John 4:10). We have recognised the communication problem that God has when He wishes to communicate with His creation and we have seen that the only way God can be appreciated by the five senses through which man perceives is when He *manifests* Himself. The only way in which He can tell humankind of the spiritual world is by *illustrating* it to us in word pictures.

There is a parallel to this in human experience. When you were a student in school or college or if you watch scientific or medical programmes on television you will know that lecturers and scientists invariably use models to help the uninitiated understand things which would otherwise be beyond their comprehension. A number of plastic balls on a piece of wire may be used to illustrate a neutron, for example. A neutron, of course, does not look at all like a collection of balls on a wire frame but at least the contraption helps us to know far more about a neutron than we did before.

More familiar, perhaps, to many of us is the ordinary charcoal, pencil or pen-and-ink drawing of a person or place.

Recently, in the course of business, I had to meet someone at a railway station, someone I had not met before. So that I could identify him he sent me a cutting from a newspaper. An article he had written was illustrated by a sketch of himself. At the station I recognised my visitor at once from the sketch.

Yet the sketch from which I had been able to recognise my visitor was, in the original, just a few pencil strokes on a piece of white paper. The sketch was quite *unlike* Mr X in so many ways. *It* was just 3in x 3in in size, *he* was over six feet tall. *It* weighed hardly anything, *he* weighed around seventeen stone. *It* was jet black and pure white, *he* was flesh coloured with rather a ruddy complexion. *It* was flat, *he* was three dimensional. The sketch was paper and printer's ink, *he* was flesh and blood.

You can probably think of a thousand ways in which that sketch differed from Mr X—yet when I saw him, I knew him immediately. I recognised him from an illustration which was in so many ways *unlike* him.

That I think is illustrative of the function of the word pictures of the Bible.

Word pictures of spiritual things

As we have seen, God has chosen to communicate with us through word pictures.

At the outset, when approaching God's illustrations of things spiritual, it is prudent to recollect and take note once more of a very important scripture: 'Now we see through a glass darkly; but then face to face; now I know in part; but then shall I know even as also I am known' (1 Corinthians 13:12).

As I have said, if you keep that scripture ever before you it will save you many a futile argument and solve many a 'mystery'.

There are several things you should not forget when looking at God's 'word pictures'.

Firstly, you should realise that He is using an experience with which you *are* familiar to illustrate something with which you are *not* familiar.

Secondly, His word pictures are 'accurate' to the extent that there is no better way the spiritual reality can be illustrated and expressed and we must therefore regard them as sacred.

Thirdly, we must *not* overliteralise such 'word pictures' because, though the picture drawn may be accurate, it will not remain accurate if pressed beyond the point it was meant to illustrate.

For example, when, at the Last Supper, Jesus said of the wine, 'This is my blood which is shed for you', and of the bread, 'This is my body which is broken for you', He was not saying that the wine was literal blood or the bread literal flesh—it could not have been because His blood was still flowing through His veins and He was still living in His body. To take His words literally would lead to all kinds of theological excess and ultimately ridicule. However, that does not mean that we should ignore the fact that Jesus was expressing a spiritual reality and that we should not treat the emblems at Holy Communion or, as some churches have it, the Lord's Table, as being the *equivalent* of the body and blood of Jesus.

Though we must *not* overliteralise such 'word pictures', hand in hand with the recognition that many of them are illustrative should go the awareness that the highest intellect in the universe has chosen those word pictures because there is no better way of saying what He wants to say and we should not therefore think of them as anything other than Divine revelation. If God *could* have found a better way of saying what He meant to say then He would have done so—if God could find no better way of describing something then we should not think that we can.

Jesus said, 'In my Father's house are many mansions.' I personally accept that! I know what a mansion is—it speaks of a grand, carefree and comfortable style of living. That is what Jesus promises believers in the afterlife. To that extent the 'many mansions' are fact. I do not feel it necessary, though, to insist that the mansions are constructed of the materials we would find in earthly mansions nor that there is a great concrete factory in eternity! Press God's word pictures beyond the point they were meant to illustrate and they cease to be applicable and become thoroughly bad and untenable theology.

We have seen in a previous chapter how when a ruler of the Jews came to Jesus, with what most people would consider to be *all* the right credentials to become a Christian, he made the mistake of overliteralising Jesus' declaration 'Ye must be born again.' Instead of getting at the nub of what Jesus was saying he began to ask Jesus how it was possible for him to return to his mother's womb. Now you see what I mean when I say that over-literalisation can make almost anything seem ridiculous!

What Jesus was saying was that it matters not how religious you are, what church you attend, how much you give to charity, how well you are thought of in your community or how well you live. There is no way in which you can comprehend God or the things appertaining to the kingdom of God until a supernatural happening has taken place in your life—until you have been initiated into the new dimension.

When you were born, you began to experience the things of this world. You did not, of course, have any consciousness of this world *before* you were conceived and very little consciousness of it while you were in the womb.

As soon as you were born you began to relate to a world which hitherto you had not known existed and to which you *could not previously relate*.

To paraphrase the saying of Jesus, 'Unless a person is born the first time he cannot *see* the kingdom of earth.'

Nicodemus, the ruler of the Jews, completely missed all that and got bogged down in thoughts about the physical impossibility of what Jesus was saying. The human mind has indeed an unfortunate habit of attaching itself to trivia!

The objective of divine revelation

The Bible was not written to tell us everything about everything, it has to do exclusively with God's dealings with the human race and the relationship of the human race to the spirit world.

Human beings have a potential affinity with both

worlds—a result of God 'breathing the breath of life into man' and man becoming a 'living soul'.

Even during our life on earth the spirit world has a profound effect on human destiny, human behaviour and human wellbeing. The Bible says:

> Put on the whole armour of God, that ye might be able to stand against the wiles of the devil. For we wrestle not against flesh and blood, but against principalities, against powers, against the rulers of darkness of this world, against spiritual wickedness in high places.
> Ephesians 6:11–12

Unless we realise that the Bible has to do exclusively with the relationship between man and the spirit world, man and God and man and man we shall expect to find answers in the Bible which are not there.

Our planet earth is, in size, but a speck in the whole of God's created universe. Because the Bible is about the God/humankind relationship, that is the confine within which the Bible is written, therefore it gives but a cursory mention of the creation of the universe and then only in so far as it affects the existence of mankind.

If you reflect on the fact that a book on carpentry will deal mainly with a little of the history of carpentry, something of the nature and characteristics of different kinds of wood, the necessary carpentry tools, the human skills appertaining to carpentry and perhaps some plans for making things out of wood—but certainly nothing to do with motor engineering—then you will see why the Bible is silent or sparse in its mention of so many subjects which interest human beings.

There is, for example, no discussion as to whether our earth was inhabited by any form of life before it 'became without form and void' nor if there are forms of life on other planets in the almost infinite depths of space. Such questions do not affect the relationship between God and Adamic man—therefore it is not the subject of God's revelation to us.

Beings that live in another dimension

We *are* told of a spirit world that exists which is *not* of this temporal world and of beings which inhabit the world, beings which exist as surely as we exist but are not flesh and blood beings as we are. It is because they from time to time have a considerable effect on life on earth and on man's relationship to God they are mentioned.

> And the angels who kept not their first estate, but left their own habitation, he hath reserved in everlasting chains under darkness unto the judgment of the great day.
> Jude 6

Unfortunately the perpetrators of religious art have chosen to depict angels as plumpish baby boys who flutter about on inadequate wings or beings similar to the fairies one is said to find at the bottom of the garden. If only, if only we humans had obeyed God's urgent injunction 'Thou shalt make unto thyself no graven image or any likeness of anything that is in heaven above or on earth beneath' we would not have such a ridiculous view of the beings the Bible speaks of as 'angels'.

Angels are spirits and, however they may manifest themselves, or be manifested at times, they have no human form. The Bible makes it plain that they have considerable influence on human activity though and that is why they are mentioned. As with so many other things given a fairly cursory mention in the Bible, cursory for the reasons I have mentioned, some expositors have taken it upon themselves to enlarge upon the knowledge the Bible gives us. Consequently many fanciful theories have emerged which find no support in the Bible.

What *kind* of beings inhabit the spirit world is something at which the Bible only hints, and then only to the extent that such beings touch upon the plan of God for human life. No great detail is given, for example, as to how that great anti-God spirit force the Bible calls 'the devil' came to be, why he is as he is or why he does what he does.

What we do know is that there *is* a great conflict in another dimension of existence and that real, thinking and purposeful influences exist which are not human and are not of God. What we know is confined to what it is *needful* for us to know and indeed, realising that spirit does not respond to the human senses, what it is *possible* for us to know.

Apart from God Himself, the Bible puts humankind at the centre of the world stage.

So let us look at how man came to be and how he came to have the relationship, or lack of it, to God that he now has—the story of the generation, degeneration and regeneration of man.

The creation of the first man Adam

> And God said, Let us make man in our image after our likeness; and let them have dominion over the fish of the sea, and over the fowl of the air, and over the cattle, and over all the earth, and over every creeping thing that creepeth upon the earth.

> So God created man in his own image, in the image of God created he him; male and female created he them.
> Genesis 1:26,27

> And the Lord God formed man of the dust of the ground, and breathed into his nostrils the breath of life; and man became a living soul. Genesis 2:7

The word 'Adam', the name by which God called the first man, simply means 'man' and, though it is given as the name of an individual in Genesis, it also stands for the whole of humankind in its 'fallen' state.

Let us look at the Genesis story—I suggest you read the first three chapters in their entirety—and realise that it is highly illustrative of spiritual truth. To argue about talking snakes, spare ribs and apples is to dwell on the trivia of the thing without appreciating that we stand in the presence of awesome truths.

The first important thing is to re-emphasise the fact that there is a great gulf fixed between the lowest forms of humankind and the highest form of animal.

There is always a danger of rejecting the Bible because of what people say it says. It is very important to read the Bible itself to see what it actually does say.

It would be easy to get sidetracked at this point in a discussion about evolution but let's resist that temptation. We'll deal a little with the evolution/creation debate in another chapter.

We need not concern ourselves too much about the actual nature of 'dust of the ground' except to say that it evidently existed *before* man was formed. We could go on for ever speculating about things like that, just as some have great fun speculating about the actual nature and chemical content of the fires of hell, but we will never know about these things because the Bible does not tell us. If God had thought it important, and in our present state of knowledge possible, for us to know then undoubtedly He *would* have told us.

Three stages of man's creation

One thing that is obvious, though, is that God formed man from an element which was already in existence and fashioned that element to His liking. *There is no statement as to how long God took to do the fashioning.*

It is, for example, perfectly acceptable if one is writing in a condensed form to write, 'Winston Churchill, who was born in Blenheim Palace, became Prime Minister of Great Britain.' *We* know that there were more than sixty years between the two events but we would not feel the need to refer to them nor would our readers assume that the two events took place on the same day or in the same year.

Having been fashioned or 'formed' of the dust of the ground, man was still not as we know him today. We are told that 'God breathed the breath of life into man and he *became* a living soul.' Man was *not* a living soul when he was formed from the 'dust of the ground' but he *became* a living soul when God breathed the breath of life into him. *There is no statement as to the time period between God forming man of the dust of the ground and man becoming a living soul.*

There are three stages of man's creation, according to the Bible the first being when God gathered together certain elements, 'the dust of the ground', which already existed *before* man was formed. The second stage was when God fashioned that dust into the form of a man. A third and final stage was when 'God breathed the breath of life into man and he became a living soul.'

You will notice from a careful reading of the creation narrative that man is the only part of the whole of creation into which 'God breathed the breath of life'. He caused other things to live but He did something very special to man.

Now, if the creation narrative has any fact in it, we would expect the lowest form of man to be different in some essential way from the rest of creation. He is!

Scientists have had to invent 'the great leap forward' to explain why no species has been found which is not wholly beast or wholly man.

All men are born with something which no animal has—a consciousness of God. It matters not how primitive the tribe, they will show their belief in an afterlife and a supreme being.

There was a time when man was very different from what he is now because, we are told, man was created in the image of God. Whether the 'image of God' referred to is a spiritual image or a physical image—though one wonders how man can have been created in the physical image of something which is not physical—matters not. What matters is that God was well satisfied with that which He had made and God is never satisfied with anything less than perfection.

In his original state man lived, a perfect being in a perfect environment. What man *became* is as a result of something that happened in his relationship with God.

Why is man inately a God-conscious being?

We have seen that though man without *the faith factor* cannot come to a knowledge of the *one true and living God* yet there is something of a 'genetic hangover' in that man has a need of a god.

One has to ask *why* all men, until they are taught to profess differently, have an instinct which causes them to believe that the human spirit survives death. There is after all no evidence easily available to the fact.

Think of the members of uncivilised tribes who see people die and witness carrion eating their flesh. Or tribes which place their dead in the trees until their bodies are rotted away—why should they think that the dead live on? The evidence of their eyes is to the contrary! Yet there is no nation or tribe which, unless taught otherwise, does not *by nature* believe that the spirit survives the body.

On the other hand, no animal has any obvious belief in life after death. While some animals and insects bury their dead it is for reasons of hygiene rather than superstition. There is little fear of a dead body discernible among animals and yet human beings, against all reason, fear the dead.

By nature human beings have a god, I write 'god' with a small 'g' advisedly, consciousness that animals do not have. Why do human beings believe in something they cannot touch, taste, see, smell or hear? Why is it they do not *stop* believing until they become 'civilised'. Mankind has to be educated into *not* believing.

The unbiased view must be, I think, that something happened way back in man's past which caused him to become a 'living soul'. It seems that the 'great leap' or 'missing link', so beloved of science, which separates man from animal by an unbridgeable gulf, and the statement that God 'breathed the breath of life into man', are one and the same thing. There *was* a great leap forward in the history of man and it was *caused* by God breathing the breath of life into him. There is no transitional species between the highest form of animal and the lowest form of man—that is fact!

Humankind loses perception of one dimension of its existence

The fall of man came about when God warned man that a certain course of action would bring both spiritual and physical death not only upon the man Adam but also upon his descendants—the Adamic race.

Evidently when God breathed the breath of life into man and man 'became a living soul' or, in other words, a spiritually responsive being, man also became vulnerable to persuasion by other spiritual entities. Even at that early stage the battle for the soul of man had begun.

The Bible says nothing about Adam and Eve eating an apple, as is so popularly thought, nor was their sin of a sexual nature.

We are told that Adam and Eve ate the fruit of a tree and the name of the tree was 'the tree of knowledge of good and evil' (Genesis 2:9).

There are those who will insist that 'the tree of the knowledge of good and evil' existed as a literal tree. To me, I say again, it matters not; I am a writer and a seeker after truth, not a botanist, and what concerns me is the message, not the literalisation of the thing. I can only say that I don't know, nor do I think that any botanist knows, of a tree of that name.

No, it matters not whether in those days one obtained the knowledge of good and evil by eating from a tree of that name, eating an apple or eating a turnip; what really matters is the obvious message to humankind and that is that, even in its perfect state, humankind was no match for the evil and supernatural 'principalities and powers' against which it fought and indeed today still fights, and that humankind was, even then, capable of obtaining more knowledge than it was morally capable of handling. Is that not the clear and discernible lesson of our present age?

Even as you are reading this book and seeing the words God has given you in His Word, 'The wages of sin is death', is there not a small voice whispering to you that you need not worry? Even as you come face to face with the dire warning of Jesus about there being a 'hell' for those who die outside of His saving grace is there not something in the back of your mind saying, 'There's nothing to worry about! When you're dead you're done for.' It's the very same voice that said to Adam, 'Thou shalt not surely die.' How can we possibly disbelieve what the Bible says happened to Adam when the same voice is denying the Word of God today and is telling us the same thing today? This is not something in the past, this is something happening in the present; this evil voice that persuaded Adam to ignore the Word of God is still doing the same thing to each and every one of us today!

Over and above *all* is the lesson that, given a free choice, Adam chose to listen to his companions, inspired by the adverse spirit the Bible calls the 'devil', rather than obey God.

It is a trait that remains with man today! But for the fact that Jesus came to *seek* and to *save* that which is lost there would none of us be saved. Whether we know it or not, it is never we who first seek God but God who first seeks us. Left to our own devices we will either follow no god or listen to false gods.

God said, 'On the day that thou eatest thereof thou shalt surely die.' The force of evil from the spirit world, the devil, through his agent, said, 'Thou shalt not surely die.' Adam believed Eve, Eve believed the serpent, the serpent believed the devil and they all blamed each other—in precisely the same way wrongdoers try to justify themselves today!

There is no great spiritual lesson to be drawn from who believed who first—they were all in it together. Neither is it a scene which has taken place only once in human history. It is the pattern of disobedience to God that everyone blames everyone else for the ills of the world.

Three happenings have been responsible for changing the destiny of the human race more than any other. The first was when man took the great leap forward from being fashioned by God of the dust of the ground to having the breath of life breathed into him. That established man as a unique creation, different fundamentally from animal.

The second happening which shaped the destiny of natural man was when the very nature of man was changed by him partaking of 'the tree of the knowledge of good and evil'.

Then was born 'the second Adam' and humankind had its chance to throw off its affinity with the old, fallen race and become members of a new human race.

> For as by one man's [Adam's] disobedience many were made sinners, so by the obedience of one [Jesus] shall many be made righteous.
>
> Romans 5:19

Now read the story of the fall of Adam and Eve again. As I have said, it would be easy for us to be sidetracked into discussing if 'the tree of knowledge of good and evil' was a real tree or if it was one of God's 'word pictures'. It really doesn't matter; what do matter are the facts that the narrative is intended to illustrate.

If we refuse to be caught in the trap of assuming that all spiritual things can be understood down to the finest detail, we can state what happened to man at the 'fall' simply and understand what happened easily.

God said 'don't' and Adam did—that is in essence what happened!

Whatever other lessons we sermonisers may draw from the narrative that lesson is central to the Garden of Eden story. It establishes precisely what sin is—*sin is disobedience to the revealed will of God.*

The punishment for sin was plainly stated before Adam sinned: 'The day that thou eatest thereof, thou shalt surely die.' That did not refer to physical death because Adam did *not* die physically that day—he *did* die towards God. He lost that part which we, because human nature became corrupt, have to have replaced by faith. The sons of Adam became the television sets not equipped with the 'other channel'.

Original sin

Evidently it was at the point at which man disobeyed God, a critical point in his development, that humankind underwent a fundamental change. The very nature of man became transformed from what it had been after God breathed the breath of life into him. Man ceased to be receptive of the truth of the one true God and ceased to be God orientated. That is not to say that man did not follow after gods of his own choosing and even of his own design. Though he had lost the part which God had put into him when He breathed the breath of life into him, the hole, the void, the place where that part had been remained, and had to be filled.

Superstition and the worship of false gods replaced the worship of the true God:

> For the invisible things of him from the creation of the world are clearly seen, being understood by the things that are made, even his eternal power and Godhead, so that they are without excuse; because when they knew God, they glorified him not as God, neither were thankful, but became vain in their imaginations, and their foolish heart was darkened.
>
> Professing themselves to be wise, they became fools, and changed the glory of the incorruptible God into an image made like corruptible man, and birds, and four-footed beasts, and creeping things.
>
> Romans 1:20–23

A change in the basic nature of humankind

It is in this concept of the change in the basic nature of man at the fall of Adam that the gospel of Jesus Christ differs from philosophical religion. The gospel of Jesus Christ proclaims that human nature became altogether corrupted at the fall. Philosophical religion, on the other hand, would teach that, given the right environment, the right education and the right religious teaching man will behave in the right way.

Philosophical religion may well use as its anthem the popular song 'Pick yourself up, dust yourself down and start all over again.' The gospel of Jesus Christ, however, despairs of fallen human nature being *able* to pull itself up by its own bootstrings and teaches that the very nature is corrupt, has to be eradicated and the person reborn. It is rebirth, re-creation and regeneration, not renovation, which Jesus came to proclaim.

I think that observation of current behaviour patterns and observation of history shows that there has been no real change in the basic nature of humankind despite our becoming much more clever, much more educated and much more informed than previous generations.

It is the *basic nature* of man that is wrong—that is the teaching of the Bible.

The corruption of human nature does not imply that all human beings behave badly all the time nor that they are actively anti-God. It implies spiritual death, spiritual blindness, spiritual unawareness and an inbuilt bias away from the revealed Word of God. It implies not so much a corruption of behaviour as a corruption of nature. It is a concept which brings us back to the premiss that natural man discerneth not the things of God—there is a part of him missing!

The concept of original sin is expressed in the following scriptures:

> Wherefore, as by one man [Adam] sin entered into the world, and death by sin, and so death passed upon *all* men, for all have sinned. Romans 5:12
>
> Nevertheless, death reigned from Adam to Moses, even over them that had *not* sinned after the similitude of Adam's transgression. Romans 5:14

It is only as our knowledge of psychology develops that we are beginning to realise that the concept of original sin is not only scriptural but scientifically acceptable. Many aspects of our behaviour *are* denominated by our instincts and instincts are genetic memory 'hand-

GENERATION—DEGENERATION—REGENERATION

downs' from previous generations. Each generation adds to the store of genetic inheritance it hands down to future generations.

There is a furore in the dog world at the moment because of the extremes to which some breeders go to breed 'desirable' traits into their dogs. Bulldogs, for example, are being bred with such big heads that bitches have difficulty in giving birth. The typical 'bulldog look' has brought about difficulty in breathing and heart trouble in many bulldogs.

It is not only physical characteristics that can be changed by breeding but also temperament and behaviour. The sheepdog has a 'built-in' behaviour pattern which makes it much more easily trained for the task of rounding-up sheep. It is also possible to breed 'good guard dog' characteristics into a line of dogs.

Of course I do not imply that the fall of Adam and the original sin which flows from it is nothing more than a 'genetic handdown' situation but what I have said *does* show that characteristics and instincts *are* passed from generation to generation. The amazing thing is that the Bible was the first book in the world to recognise the fact!

Why should we, then, find it so unusual a proposition that a propensity for sin was genetically programmed into human beings by one man's actions?

Even the Apostle Paul said of himself:

> For I know that in me (that is in my flesh) dwelleth no good thing; for to will is present with me, but how to perform that which is good I find not. For the good that I would I do not; but the evil which I would not, that I do. Now if I do that I would not,

> it is no more I that do it, but sin that dwelleth in me.
> Romans 7:18–20

We have all had *that* experience. Human beings have, by nature, a certain predisposition for sin. There is still, in the best of us, the warring of the flesh and the spirit.

Let us look at the proposition that man is afflicted by original sin from an experimental point of view. After thousands of years of religion, philosophy and education does it not strike you as being odd that human beings still do such unbelievably cruel things to each other? Do we not see the evidence of original sin all around us? There is a very definite bias towards doing wrong in mankind. Despite the care with which we apply the veneer to our civilisation do we not quite regularly see the old chipboard showing through?

Total corruption

Many people misunderstand what is meant by the Christian doctrine of the total corruption of human nature. They take it to mean that there is nothing good about human nature. That is not what the doctrine means at all.

A few weeks ago I had the warning 'File corrupted' flash on my computer screen. What it meant was that in certain specific ways that file would no longer respond to my commands. I sought through the file until I came to the point at which it was 'corrupted' and, when I had removed the corruption, I was able to command the situation again. The communication which had been lost between the computer and myself was restored.

Though that file was not *all* corrupt it was *totally* corrupt in the sense that until I undertook the work of rectification on it I could not communicate with it and it could not communicate with me. There was no great blemish on the disk, perhaps a mere speck of dust, but that speck of dust was enough to stop the thing working altogether.

The warning of 'corruption' at no time meant that there was *nothing* useful in the file nor that everything which emanated from that file was corrupt.

When we speak of a person as being 'dead in trespasses and sin' we do not infer that the person of whom we speak is a wholly bad person. Indeed, though it should *not* be so, it is a fact that cannot be denied that many people who are 'dead in trespasses and sin' live better lives than do some Christians. Nevertheless, though their lives are exemplary, they will be unable to come to a true knowledge of God because they are 'dead [to God] in trespasses and sin'.

To go back to our illustration of the television set. Though the cabinet may be a work of craftsmanship and the tube give a brilliant picture, though the sound clarity is sparkling and the set be made by one of the top manufacturers in the world, none of that will help the set to receive the channel you want it to receive if it is not equipped to do so.

Whereas, before his disobedience, Adam had had intimate communion with God, we find a very different picture *after* he had disobeyed God.

We now read of Adam walking in the garden in the cool of the day when God spoke to him. The lesson is that Adam no longer knew that God was present—God now had to communicate with *him* to make His presence known. Adam's reaction was the reaction of a guilty man—he hid himself from God. From then on neither Adam nor the descendants of Adam would, of their own volition, seek the one true and living God, preferring to hide themselves behind gods and contrivances of their own choosing.

I could write a volume on the way I have seen men and women hide from God—I have even seen people hide from God behind a cloak of virtue!

An irrevocable law

When I am challenged by people who say that there is something unfair about people being condemned by original sin I ask the question 'Can *you* personally say that you have not done precisely what Adam did?' I have not met one person who could say that they have never sinned in their life. So there's nothing really unfair about it because all of us have committed Adam's sin by contravening the commands of God at some time during our lives. If Adam had not done it for us we would most certainly have done it for ourselves!

'But,' someone will say, 'there *is* unfairness in the fact that I have these spiritual impediments, this bias towards sin and this corrupt nature with which I was burdened at birth.'

There is no unfairness because, though you may have had no say in the fact that you were born with the taint of Adam's transgression upon you, it is you who choose to *keep* that taint. Jesus says you can be *born again* and take on a new nature—you can rid yourself of Adam's curse. So though you were not able to avoid *having* it, you can most certainly avoid *keeping* it!

> The wages of sin is death, but the gift of God is eternal life through Jesus Christ our Lord.
> Romans 6:23

> As in Adam all die, even so in Christ shall all be made alive.   1 Corinthians 15:12

The choice you have to make is whether you will remain 'in Adam' or choose to be 'in Christ'—the choice is yours and the responsibility is yours!

Sin is—not obeying the rules

If you think about it for a moment you will appreciate that spiritual death is the unavoidable consequence of sin. Even *human* society cannot exist unless we take those who transgress its laws out of circulation.

We have living proof in our own society that as law and order becomes more relaxed the lives of all of us become less free. Time was when folk could walk the streets in safety but time was too when the felon was severely punished for his crime. When the rules are broken 'the game' becomes unplayable.

A simple game of football could not be played unless there were rules and the rules would not be of use if it was left to everyone's discretion whether or not they kept them. There has therefore to be a system by which those who obey the rules are allowed to play whilst those who break the rules are sent off the field.

I am a company chairman by profession. I know that my company will not do very well if everyone in it ignores the rules and does what they want to do, so I have to have a method by which those who, after fair warning, refuse to keep the rules are removed from the company. It would be unfair to those who depend on the company for their living, it would be unfair to my customers and it would also mean that *I was company chairman in name only* if I allowed those who refused to keep the rules to remain!

That brings me to the point that it is not always a simple matter of judging how harmful a single act of breaking the law is. Parking one's car in a no-parking zone may, as an isolated act, not harm anyone very much. Yet if it is *allowed* to happen once then others will park their cars in an exclusion zone and traffic congestion will result. Ultimately, if no action is taken to enforce the law and everyone begins to park their cars where it pleases them then movement in the city will, at certain times, become impossible. So a simple act of law breaking which the perpetrator may have considered did not 'do anyone any harm' could cause mayhem. Yet the punishment of one person for leaving their car in an exclusion zone may seem authoritarian and heavy handed if not seen in the context of the overall need to apply a general rule.

There are rules in our society for the safety and well-being of the individual. Specialists in fire prevention frame the rules which are enforced in public buildings and the owners of the buildings sometimes consider some of the rules to be the product of too much officialdom. That is often because they are not specialists in fire prevention, they have no special knowledge of how fires start, how fire spreads and how it may be most effectively contained after it has started. Their lack of knowledge is *not* in itself dangerous, indeed, it is knowledge that the ordinary person cannot be expected to have because not everyone can be an expert in every subject.

As long as we are prepared to *obey the rules laid down by others who do know* no harm will result from our lack of knowledge. Similarly, we cannot be expected to understand fully the workings and the prohibitions which apply to the spirit world and that which is spirit. Our only defence is to obey the instructions of He who knows, without question.

For example, no one when the Scripture was written 3,500 years ago would think God's food law 'Ye shall eat no manner of fat' (Leviticus 7:23) to be anything other than one of those peculiar things which God from time to time instructed them to obey. Why not eat fat? Well, in the past ten or so years we have come to *know why* we should not eat fat. In an age when no one knew anything about 'cholesterol levels' it must have seemed rather a silly rule.

Of course the stability of the British nation, the stability of a game of football and the stability of my companies pale into insignificance when compared to the magnitude of the organisation of life on planet earth and in the spirit world. Let me suggest to you that if God let disobedience go unchecked He would no longer be God because other, lesser and more perverse wills would be challenging Him for supremacy. *The very concept of God demands that His will is enforced.*

Excommunication from the presence of God

God did not strike Adam with physical death but rather with excommunication from His presence and the inability to perceive spiritual things (spiritual death). Had God not blighted mankind with spiritual death it is probable mankind would have brought the spiritual world to the brink of destruction.

We see this idea in the words recorded in the Garden of Eden story when God said after the fall of Adam, 'Man has become as one of us. Let us guard the way of the tree of life lest he should partake thereof and live forever.' Can you imagine the world with a couple of everlasting Hitlers in it? If we survey the panorama of history I think we should be pleased that the world has been relieved of the antics of some of its worst citizens by—*death!*

It's worth noticing especially the words spoken by God: 'And the Lord God said, Behold, the man is become as one of us' (Genesis 3:22). It is one of the most profound prophecies of the Old Testament. There was little in primitive man to substantiate the view that 'man has become as one of us'. What could be considered Godlike about the man who God had to clothe with coats of skin?

Looking at man today as he walks on the surface of the moon, sends probes into outer space, stands on the brink of being able to 'make' different kinds of animals in the laboratory and is able even to 'tailor-make' human beings if he were permitted to do so, the proposition that 'man has become one of us' seems altogether reasonable.

There are few, I think, except perhaps on the outer fringes of science, who do not stand in both awe and horror at the capabilities of man, and few would argue with me when I suggest that it is altogether desirable that someone has put a curb on this creature, man, whose ability seems (other than by outside intervention) to have no bounds. We have seen in the too recent past in Nazi Germany, the Soviet Union and other countries what can happen to society when the forces of perverted science are unleashed.

Yes, man *has* become as God! I, as a Christian, am not surprised at the capability of man to do all the things he is doing. Nothing of what is happening in science today shakes my faith at all—why should it? After all, it *was* God Himself who said—when there was little evidence for the proposition at the very beginning of man's existence—'he has become one of us.'

The great blockage

So spiritual death is the great blockage put there by God to preserve His own supremacy and to ensure that man's godlike qualities are not extended to the spiritual realm.

We humans know about banishing things from our presence and sometimes sentencing them to death in the process. Our health services spend a lot of money on antibiotics to destroy those things which bring about a state of illness in our bodies. Not only that but our bodies have naturally formed antibodies which drive out disease. Had we not got such defences we would probably die of the common cold.

Sin is to God and the spiritual environment what the deadly virus is to the human body. The very perfection of God demands that it be driven from His presence. For God to tolerate sin would be a change of His most fundamental characteristic—holiness.

It is not until we realise the abhorrence that God has towards sin that we realise how impossible it is for Him to countenance it. Of course, it is very difficult for us to understand how hateful sin is to God because, as I have said, He is a Spirit and we do not understand the environment in which a spirit exists but, as is the function of parable, we shall relate it to things we *do* understand.

We will not allow animals which are incapable of being house trained into our houses because our standards of hygiene will simply not allow us to tolerate it.

That is not to say that the animal is not behaving perfectly within its own idea of what is right and what is wrong—nevertheless we banish it from our presence.

Vicious dogs are sentenced to death because we know the damage they can do those with whom they come in contact. The dog may be vicious with the best of motives, to protect itself from real or imaginary threat or even think it is protecting us, but that doesn't matter to us! Unless the dog will become trained (obey our commandments) then it has to go.

You do not knowingly allow wild cats into your house because you know they will attack you and your family, destroy your home and perhaps spread disease. They will also cause the place to stink with an odour which does not upset them and which they do not notice but which does upset you and which you notice very much indeed! You know too that they will breed until they have overrun the place. So you either exclude them from your home or tame them.

Excluding them from your home means that you are refusing them admission into your presence and the corollary of that is that future generations of wild cats will grow up either not knowing you exist or only catching glimpses of you—they will not have a relationship with you.

Taming them will involve a system of reward and punishment which will ultimately cause them to *do your will*.

I wonder if the ordinary mouse understands why we humans kill it? Does it not behave honourably by its own standards? Is it not obeying the dictates of the nature which is within it? Could it not claim to work hard, looking after its young, feeding them and housing them to the best of its ability? For these, as it would seem to the mouse, virtues we trap it and kill it! It does not understand what its good intentions do to *our* 'kingdom' otherwise it would understand!

That may help you to grasp, in some small degree, why God excommunicated mankind from His presence. A warning, though, as with any other parable: do not push the illustration too far otherwise you'll have a brand new religion on your hands.

The earthy and the heavenly

> And so it is written, The first man Adam was made a living soul; the last Adam [Jesus] was made a life-giving spirit. However, that was not first which was spiritual, but that which was natural; and afterward that which is spiritual.
>
> The first man is of the earth, earthy; the second man is the Lord from heaven.
>
> As is the earthy, such are they also that are earthy; and as is the heavenly, such are they also that are heavenly.
>
> And as we have borne the image of the earthy, we shall also bear the image of the heavenly. Now this I say, brethren, that flesh and blood cannot inherit the kingdom of God; neither doth corruption inherit incorruption.   1 Corinthians 15:45–50

The choice is yours! To remain in that family into which you were born—the earthly family of the first man Adam—or to be *born again* into the heavenly family of the second Adam, the Lord Jesus Christ, and enter *the new dimension of life.*

11 *The Coming of the Saviour*

AT THIS POINT you will probably have realised that there is far more to the story of Jesus of Nazareth than you had hitherto contemplated.

I would imagine that, if you have called upon the name of the Lord as I have outlined in previous chapters, Jesus has by now been revealed to you as the Christ the Son of the living God by *the faith factor*, the inner witness, a higher intellect than human intellect. You will probably already have passed from unawareness of, rejection of or mere intellectual assent to the historic person of Jesus to a living faith.

Whilst *the faith factor* is sufficient for us, for with the hymnwriter we can say 'I need no other argument, I need no other plea', the Bible says that we should always be prepared to give a reason for the hope that is within us: 'Be ready always to give an answer to every man that asketh you a reason for the hope that is in you' (1 Peter 3:15). So I would like to 'back up' your faith with some

THE COMING OF THE SAVIOUR

rather unusual, one might almost say 'mysterious', facts about Jesus.

Of course you will know, if only from the Christmas cards you receive and the Christmas carols you sing at Christmas time, that Jesus was born in Bethlehem of the Virgin Mary. I hope to show you that there is much more to the Christmas story than that! In fact I think I can promise you that, when you have read this chapter, Christmas will never be quite the same again. You will realise the full extent of the miraculous event which took place in the year 7 BC and appreciate that it was not some random event but the culmination of a long-term plan of God.

I want to take you to a road just outside the town of Emmaus which is not far from Jerusalem and let you listen to a little bit of conversation which took place between Jesus and two Emmaus disciples.

The crucifixion and the resurrection are in the recent past and it is the *risen* Christ who speaks to His disciples.

> Then he [Jesus] said unto them, O foolish ones, and slow of heart to believe all that the prophets have spoken!
> Ought not the Christ to have suffered these things, and to enter into his glory? *And beginning at Moses and all the prophets, he expounded to them, in all the scriptures, the things concerning himself.* Luke 24:25–27

The scriptures of which He spoke were of course those writings which we now call the Old Testament. Some of them had been written hundreds and some of them thousands of years before He was born, yet, He claimed, they spoke of Him! Now I think you will agree that is rather an unusual claim for anyone to make.

Whenever Jesus was asked to give temporal proof of His claim to be the Messiah He turned to Bible prophecy and showed how the predictions of the ancient prophets had been fulfilled in Himself.

Let us look at some of the circumstances which surrounded the birth of Jesus.

'Virgin births' were not all that unusual

We must remember that at the time of the birth of Jesus the penalty for fornication or adultery was death. It was not unusual therefore for an unmarried young lady expecting a child to look for some other explanation for her unfortunate condition. In that age of mysticism, God was often blamed, as He is now, for things for which He was not responsible.

The rulers of the day didn't take too much notice of such 'virgin births' because, not only was it not an unusual claim for someone to make, 'virgin births' were no particular threat to their authority.

That's why the reaction of King Herod was so unusual at the time of the birth of Jesus! It was recognised, even at the time and among the highest rulers in the land, that there was something very unusual about the birth of Jesus.

We read in the Gospel according to Saint Matthew words which, unfortunately, few people dwell deeply upon.

> When Herod, the king, had heard these things, *he was troubled and all Jerusalem with him*. And when he had gathered all the chief priests and scribes of

THE COMING OF THE SAVIOUR

the people together, he demanded of them where Christ should be born. And they said unto him, In Bethlehem of Judaea; for thus it is written by the prophet.   Matthew 2:3–5

We read that Herod was troubled and all Jerusalem with him! Why should the mighty Herod be troubled about a baby born in a manger? Can you imagine the President of the United States of America getting hot under the collar about a baby born in a cattle shed in a country district in America? Can you imagine the Prime Minister of Great Britain becoming very 'troubled' because a girl in Broadstairs had claimed to have had a virgin birth?

The answer is 'yes', assuming that the circumstances surrounding the birth of the child were similar to those surrounding the birth of Jesus.

I must make the point here that I am depending on evidence *external* to the Bible as well as evidence *internal* in the Bible.

The evidence of astronomy

Jesus was born in very unusual circumstances indeed!

Let me take you back, by relatively recently discovered facts of astronomy, to the time of Jesus.

We are inclined to think that knowledge of the birth of Jesus was confined to a rather small area around Bethlehem but that is not so. There is evidence to suggest that at the time of the birth of Jesus, and for several months before, *the whole of the Middle East was in a ferment of expectation of the coming of the world deliverer!*

In those days there were important schools of astrology in Jerusalem and in other major centres of the Middle East. Some of their records have been brought to light recently and they show that the birth of a very important person was to be expected in 7 BC.

I do not want to digress but someone will no doubt point out that Jesus was *not* born in 7 BC but in AD 1. Well that is not so. The Bible tells us that Jesus was born 'in the days of Herod the king'. We know that Herod died in 4 BC.

The fact is that the AD dates have nothing to do with the Bible record. The AD system of dating is inaccurate: it is a system of dating that owes little to the birth of Christ and rather more to the imagination, and the poor mathematics, of a Scythian monk Dionysius Exiguus who was instructed in AD 533 to commence a new calendar working backwards from his day to the birth of Christ. As was to be expected, he was years adrift in his reckoning.

Between the birth of Jesus and the death of Herod there were three events which would have taken at least three years. There was the completion of the census during which 'the whole world' was to be taxed—not something which would be completed very quickly. There was the slaughter of the innocents and there was the flight into Egypt.

The mysterious conjunction in the heavens

Herod was troubled! And well might he be for astrologers, of many different faiths and nations, were in agreement that an event of great portent was about to happen in Israel.

The Jewish rabbinical writer Abarbanel had maintained that the Messiah would appear when there was a conjunction of the stars Jupiter and Saturn. According to Jewish tradition *Jupiter* was thought of as the *kingly star* and *Saturn* was *the protector of Israel.* Saturn was regarded by certain non-Jewish astronomers as being the star of *the God of the Jews!*

It is against this background that we must read the narrative of the birth of Jesus. It was not an insignificant event taking place in a manger in Bethlehem but something of an international event.

The evidence of an imperial mathematician

There lived in the early 1600s in Prague an imperial mathematician and Astronomer Royal by the name of Johannes Kepler.

On the night of December 17th, over 1,600 years after the birth of Jesus, Kepler had his telescope trained on the heavens, for he knew that an exceptional event was to take place: Saturn and Jupiter were to enter a conjunction in the constellation of Pisces.

A 'conjunction', as far as the layman is concerned, merely means the position of two stars on the same degree of longitude.

As Kepler watched, the two stars seemed to come closer together until all he could see in the sky was one bright star of wonderful brilliance. Probably the awe-inspiring sight was the reason his mind leapt back to something he had read years before but had forgotten until that moment—the prophecy of the writer Abarbanel that the Messiah would appear when there was a conjunction of Saturn and Jupiter in the constellation of Pisces.

In his planetarium Kepler 'turned the heavens back'

over 1,600 years and checked and rechecked his calculations. He thrilled with excitement when he found that the same conjunction of the stars Jupier and Saturn had occurred in the constellation of Pisces in the year 7-6 BC.

Ancient Babylonian records deciphered—1925

It was to be over 300 years before Kepler's findings were confirmed. In 1925 a German by the name of Schnabel deciphered the records of a famous school of astrology that had existed in Babylon in ancient times; the school was the School of Astrology at Sippar in Babylon. Among the mine of information he found proof that Jupier and Saturn had been in conjunction in the constellation of Pisces in the year 7 BC!

Kepler had been right, Jupiter and Saturn *did* meet in Pisces three times in the year 7 BC.

The events of 7 BC

Remember what the astrologers of the ancient world believed that the three stars which met in conjunction in the year 7 BC signified:

> Jupiter—the Kingly star.
> Saturn—the protector of Israel.
> Pisces—the sign of the Messiah.

You can imagine can't you how the civilised world would be holding its breath with excitement as the time for the conjunction approached.

In addition to the portentious stars there was the ancient writ which contained many predictions of seers concerning the coming of the Messiah-God. The predic-

THE COMING OF THE SAVIOUR

tion of the prophet Micah, 'But thou Bethlehem Ephratah, though thou be little among the thousands of Judah, yet out of thee shall he come forth unto me that is to be ruler in Israel, whose goings forth have been from of old, from everlasting' (Micah 5:2), would be known to them.

That prediction about the coming of the Messiah had been written hundreds of years before the conjunction of the stars was due to take place.

Thus the 'wise men', 'Magi' or 'Astrologers' would know exactly *where* the birth of the Messiah-King would take place and all they had to do was to look for 'His star' and they would know the time of His coming.

The message of the stars was so powerful that no astrologer could ignore it: 'The King star'. 'The protector of Israel star' were to come together in the constellation of 'The sign of the Messiah star'.

At the very end of February in the year 7 BC, the ancient astronomers watched the heavens, undoubtedly with the writing of the prophets open before them, as Jupiter moved into the constellation of Pisces and towards Saturn—what was about to happen was long awaited and significant, the most significant astrological event in the history of mankind.

Further conjunctions took place on April 12th and on May 29th and on December 4th of 7 BC. Jupiter and Saturn met in the constellation of Pisces for the last time. The conjunction, or as we know it, *the star of Bethlehem* had shed its light on humanity.

History too attests to the fact that the coming of Jesus was proclaimed in the heavens. Flavius Josephus, the ancient Jewish historian, tells us that at the time of the birth of Jesus it was said in Jerusalem that there had been a sign in the heavens proclaiming the birth of a Jewish king.

That is why Herod was troubled! The whole of the astrological world of the Middle East was expecting the birth of the Messiah immediately prior to the birth of Jesus.

The coming of the Messiah-God

Herod would have been aware of who and what the Messiah/God was to be. The idea of the coming of the Messiah was not something which was introduced when Jesus was born, it was the long expected hope of all Israel.

We must never think of Christianity as being a *new* religion which started with the birth of Jesus. Christianity is the natural unfolding of the religion of the Old Testament. As someone has well said, 'The New is in the Old concealed—the Old is in the New revealed.' Jesus Christ was the fulfilment of the many promises, which we find throughout the Old Testament, of the coming of the deliverer.

A careful reading of His life story will show you that Jesus continued to worship in the Temple and the Synagogue, as did His disciples.

It may be difficult sometimes to see in the Old Testament religion a resemblance to the religion of the New Testament but you may reflect upon the fact that an acorn does not look at all like an oak tree yet the one is the source of the other.

It is only because Christianity is sometimes taken in isolation, largely divorced from the teaching of the Old Testament, that there is a debate in the church about whether or not Jesus was God.

THE COMING OF THE SAVIOUR

To the prophets of ancient Israel the coming of the Messiah-God was the most important of events. No one in those days would have subscribed to the view held by some theologians that the Messiah was to be simply an earthly deliverer, a supreme leader or an ordinary king. They were in no doubt whatsoever that the Messiah was to be Jehovah (one of the names for God) Himself.

As we have seen, the prophet Isaiah made his expectations as to the identity of the Messiah quite plain when he wrote around 700 BC:

> For unto us a child is born, unto us a son is given, and the government shall be upon his shoulder; and his name shall be called Wonderful Counsellor, *The Mighty God, The Everlasting Father,* The Prince of Peace. Isaiah 9:6

So when Jesus claimed to be the Messiah He was undoubtedly claiming to be *'The Mighty God'* and *'The Everlasting Father'*. When Peter confessed that Jesus was 'the Christ' he too was attesting that Jesus was *'The Mighty God'* and *'The Everlasting Father'*.

When Herod heard from the astronomers that the Messiah was to be born he would expect the child to be none other than the Messiah-God. Little wonder he was troubled!

The coming of the Messiah-God in prophecy

There are several things we should keep in mind as we read the prophecies regarding the coming of Jesus the Christ. The first thing to remember is that, at the time it was written, at least two-thirds of the Bible was written to foretell future events. Among those future events none was given more prominence than the coming of Jesus.

Remember too that the Old Testament, in which we find the prophecies regarding the coming of the Messiah, has always been in the custodianship of the Jewish people. We should be grateful to them for the integrity with which they kept the Scriptures.

It is obvious that the Jews had no interest in proving Jesus to be the Messiah and so we can feel confident that the prophecies regarding Jesus in the Old Testament have not been tampered with to prove His Messiahship and are there as they were originally written.

The family into which the Messiah would be born foretold

Some 800 years *before* Jesus was born, the ancient prophet Isaiah wrote:

> And there shall come forth a rod out of the stem of Jesse, and a Branch shall grow out of his roots; and the spirit of the Lord shall rest upon him, the spirit of wisdom and understanding, the spirit of counsel and might, the spirit of knowledge and of fear of the Lord.
> Isaiah 11:1,2

Eight hundred years after that prophecy had been written Jesus was born of the family line of Jesse precisely as predicted!

The place the Messiah would be born foretold

Had we not got the benefit of hindsight we might well think that the prophets had spoken in a contradictory

THE COMING OF THE SAVIOUR

way. The prophecies concerning Jesus are littered with what, at the time, would have seemed contradictions.

Had there been collusion between the ancient seers and had there been collusion between those who subsequently had custody of the Scriptures they would have doubtless changed the text so that one prophet did not appear to contradict another.

It is an attestation of the faith both of the writers and the custodians of the Old Testament that they kept the record exactly as it had been uttered even though it did not, at the time, seem to make sense.

Writings at about the same time as Isaiah the prophet Hosea looked forward to the coming of the Messiah and wrote:

> Out of Egypt have I called my son. Hosea 11:1

A prophet of whom *we* have no record, but whose utterances were evidently well known in Palestine at the time of Christ, foretold that the Messiah would be a Nazarene (be of the town of Nazareth)—see Matthew 2:23.

Yet another prophet, Micah, writing in the eighth century BC, foretold that the Messiah would come out of Bethlehem:

> But thou, Bethlehem Ephratah, though thou be little among the thousands of Judah, yet out of thee shall he come forth unto me that is to be ruler in Israel, whose goings forth have been from of old, from everlasting. Micah 5:2

Three different prophets, writing at different times and predicting three different origins for the Messiah

God. One prophet foretold the Messiah would come from Bethlehem, another from Egypt and a third from Nazareth.

The story of Jesus is too well known for me to elaborate on it here. In hindsight we know, as no one who lived *before* the event could possibly have known, that all three of the ancient seers were correct.

Mary and Joseph had their home in Nazareth, and Jesus was therefore entitled to be called a 'Nazarene'.

Just prior to the birth of Jesus, Caesar Augustus sent out an edict that 'all the world' should be taxed, and as Mary and Joseph were passing through, travelling for the purpose of obeying the edict, Jesus was born in Bethlehem.

When Herod heard of the birth of Jesus he ordered a 'slaughter of the innocents' causing the family of Jesus to flee and take Jesus into Egypt.

All the prophets proved to be correct regarding the place to which the Messiah would come.

The coming of the King foretold

Can you imagine how Zechariah felt when, 500 years before the birth of Jesus, he was called upon by the Lord to predict regarding the coming of the God-King of Israel.

Kings in those days were not the democratic constitutional monarchs we know today. The king was the centre of pomp and ceremony and had the power of life and death over his people. Being a king was essentially ballyhoo: the more high and mighty, the more elaborate, the more finely clad and jewel bedecked the king, the further his fame spread. But the Israelites were not expecting an ordinary king; they were expecting He who was to become *King of all the earth*.

THE COMING OF THE SAVIOUR 191

Human nature must have fought a tremendous battle within Zechariah when he was called upon to write something that would seem ridiculous to him.

> Rejoice greatly, O daughter of Zion; shout, O daughter of Jerusalem: behold, thy King cometh unto thee; he is just and having salvation; lowly, and riding upon an ass, and upon a colt, the foal of an ass.
> Zechariah 9:9

No mighty leader at the head of a conquering army? No pomp and no ceremony? The God-King of Israel and the whole world 'lowly'? How can this be? Riding on an ass? Surely nonsense!

Five hundred years roll by and Zechariah is long dead but his prophecy has not been forgotten for it is read avidly in Jewish places of worship. How many *really* believe it will ever happen? Five hundred years is a long time, people give up hope!

Come stand with me 500 years after the prophet had made his prediction. We are standing at the foot of the Mount of Olives and, in the distance, we hear cheering and rejoicing. Into view comes a procession, people are throwing branches and leaves in the path of a man riding, incongruously, on an ass. The man is none other than Jesus of Nazareth. Read the report of what happened to Jesus and then read again the prophecy of Zechariah:

> And [the disciples] brought the ass, and the colt, and put on them their clothes, and they sat him [Jesus] thereon. And a very great multitude spread their garments in the way; others cut down branches from the trees, and spread them in the

way. And the multitudes that went before, and that followed, cried, saying, Hosanna to the Son of David! Blessed is he that cometh in the name of the Lord! Hosanna in the highest!   Matthew 21:7–9

The betrayal of the Messiah-God foretold

Prophecy took several forms and before we read the next prophecy let me mention just two.

The first method by which prophetic knowledge was given was when the prophet saw a vision or heard a voice. The second form is that in which the voice of the originator of the message speaks in the first person *through* the prophet.

King David of Israel received many of the second type of prophecies in which the originator of the prophecy, 'the Lord', spoke directly through him rather as a loudspeaker of a radio is used to relay the voice of a broadcaster. Such is the prophecy we are about to examine.

It is the Messiah-God speaking through Zechariah 500 years before He came to earth:

> And I said unto them, If ye think good, give me my price; and if not, forbear. So they weighed for my price *thirty pieces of silver*. And the Lord said unto me, Cast it unto the potter: a goodly price I was prised at of them. And I took the thirty pieces of silver, and cast them to the potter in the house of the Lord.   Zechariah 11:12,13

Three things the Messiah, speaking through the voice of Zechariah, foretold about Himself over 500 years before it happened:

THE COMING OF THE SAVIOUR

1. The exact price of His betrayal!
2. The money would be cast to 'the potter'!
3. The place it would be cast to the potter was to be 'in the house of the Lord'!

It seems nonsensical doesn't it? You would think that sensible Rabbis would have tried to alter it and make some sense of it. But, as usual, nobody tried to alter the words of the prophet.

Let us read the record of the events of the betrayal of Jesus:

> Then Judas, which had betrayed him, when he saw that he [Jesus] was condemned, repented himself, and brought again the *thirty pieces of silver* to the chief priests and elders saying, I have sinned in that I have betrayed innocent blood. And they said, What is that to us?... And he cast down the pieces of silver *in the temple* [the house of the Lord], and departed, and went and hanged himself. And the chief priests took the pieces of silver, and said, It is not lawful to put them in the treasury, because it is the price of blood. And they took counsel, and bought with them the *potter's field*.
> Matthew 27:3–8

Once again we see the most unlikely prediction come to pass. It came to pass over 500 years after it had been uttered. It came to pass accurately in every detail!

- Exactly thirty pieces of silver as the voice speaking through Zechariah had said.
- Cast down in the house of the Lord as had been predicted.

- Finally used to purchase the 'potter's field'.

The fulfilment is all the more amazing when it is realised that the 'potter's field' which was purchased with the money was not known by that name until long after the prophecy had been uttered. Not only did the 'voice' predict what would be done with the money but the name that would be given to the field 450 years hence!

The voice of the Messiah foretelling His future betrayal through King David adds to the betrayal narrative when it says:

> Yea, mine own familiar friend, in whom I trusted, who did eat of my bread, hath lifted up his heel against me.   Psalm 41:9

- The Messiah-God was to be betrayed by someone who was His own familiar friend.
- The betrayal would happen through a man who had 'eaten bread' with the Messiah.

The story is too well known for me to labour the point. Judas was a close friend of Jesus and ate with Him at the last supper. The prophecy came to pass quite literally and in every detail at the betrayal of Jesus!

The death of the Messiah-God foretold

As I have previously remarked, the coming of the Messiah was considered among the Jews to be a time of deliverance for their nation, a time when peace would be ushered in and their God take the throne of their father David and rule for ever. It is astonishing, therefore, that any prophet dared to foretell or any scribe record a

THE COMING OF THE SAVIOUR

prophecy of the *death* of the Messiah-God. It is also astonishing that such a prediction should be retained in the annals of Jewish prophecy.

A 'prophecy' devised of the human mind would have predicted an all-conquering Messiah and the subjugation of Israel's enemies. The death of the eternal Messiah-God would seem to be a contradiction in terms of such an inventive mind, yet through King David came the prophecy in 1000 BC.

> I am poured out like water, and all my bones are out of joint: my heart is like wax; it is melted within me.
>
> My strength is dried up like a potsherd, and my tongue cleaveth to my jaws; and thou hast brought me into the dust of death.
>
> For dogs have compassed me; the assembly of the wicked have enclosed me; *they pierced my hands and my feet*.
>
> I may count all my bones; they look and stare upon me.
>
> They parted my garment among them, and cast lots upon my vesture.   Psalm 22:14–18

To appreciate how wonderful that prophecy really is you have to realise that when it was written *crucifixion was not practised in Israel;* the death penalty, as carried out in the land of Israel in those days, was stoning to death. Look as you will through the Old Testament, you will not find any reference to death by crucifixion. Yet, looking forward to His coming to earth, the Messiah was, through the mouth of David, able to describe the crucifixion scene 1,000 years before it happened!

Even the minutest detail of the grim crucifixion scene

was foretold, 1,000 years before it was enacted on Golgotha.

What of the time between the betrayal and the crucifixion? Had the prophets anything to say about that? Yes, 700 years before the event Isaiah had prophesied:

> He was oppressed, and he was afflicted, yet he opened not his mouth; he is brought as a lamb to the slaughter, and as a sheep before the shearers is dumb, so he opened not his mouth.   Isaiah 53:7

Now read the eye-witness account of how Jesus behaved when he was before Pontius Pilate on the judgement day:

> When he was accused of the chief priests and elders, he answered them nothing. Then said Pilate unto him, Hearest thou not how many things they witness against thee? and he answered him never a word.   Matthew 27:12–14

The Messiah, speaking through Isaiah, 700 years before He came to earth said:

> I gave my back to the smiters...I hid not my face from shame and spitting.   Isaiah 50:6

Read what the prophet Micah foretold 800 years before Christ was condemned:

> They shall strike the judge of Israel with a rod upon the cheek.   Micah 5:1

THE COMING OF THE SAVIOUR

Now read Matthew's account of the events after Jesus' arrest:

> And they spit upon him, and took the reed and smote him on the head. Matthew 27:30

Read John's account:

> Pilate took Jesus and scourged him. John 19:1

The ancient seers said that the Messiah-God would:

- Be smitten on the back.
- Be hit on the cheek with a rod.
- Have His face spat on.

The prophecies were fulfilled in Jesus of Nazareth! Speaking through King David 1,000 years before the event the Messiah-God foretold:

> False witnesses did rise up; they laid things to my charge that I knew not. Psalm 35:11

Here's the contemporary account of what happened to Jesus:

> The chief priests, and elders, and all the council, sought false witness against Jesus, to put him to death. Matthew 26:59

Who was it whom the prophetic scriptures foretold. He would be spat upon, smitten, humiliated and crucified? None other than the Messiah, the Mighty God, the Everlasting Father, the Prince of Peace. Could anything more unlikely be foretold of such a person? Could human mind devise such seemingly ridiculous prophecies? Prophecies of the conquering hero, yes; prophecies of a successful revolutionary leader, yes, or prophecies of a King mighty in war, yes, but, as I have said, it would take either a lunatic or an inspired man to foretell this complete humiliation even unto death of the Messiah-God.

Think for a moment. If you were asked to write a story about a God-King would you write things like that?

The unusual circumstances of Jesus' burial in prophecy

Isaiah, writing many thousands of years before the birth of Christ, predicted the circumstances in which Jesus would be buried:

> He was taken from prison and from judgement; and who shall declare his generation? For he was cut off out of the land of the living; for the transgression of my people was he stricken. And he made his grave with the *wicked*, and with the rich in his death. Isaiah 53:8,9

It is not the kind of thing the human mind would devise to say about the coming Messiah but, once again, we see the unlikely come to pass. Jesus *was* crucified between two thieves and He *was* buried in a rich man's tomb.

Predicting the death of the Messiah 1,000 years before the event King David wrote:

> He keepeth all his bones, not one of them is broken.
> Psalm 34:20

It was usual for the soldiers to break the legs of a crucified person and so they did to the thieves on either side of Jesus but they *did not* break any bone in Jesus' body.

> Then came the soldiers, and broke the legs of the first, and of the other who was crucified with him. But when they came to Jesus, and saw that he was dead already, they broke not his legs.
> John 19:32,33

That is a much more significant happening than would at first appear. It was the teaching of the ancient prophets that the Messiah would be a sacrificial lamb for the nation and the individual as the Passover lamb had been those many years before. Hence the saying of John the Baptist when he baptised Jesus:

> Behold the Lamb of God, which taketh away the sins of the world.
> John 1:29

One of the rules regarding the sacrificial lamb was that *no bone of it was to be broken!*

Meditate upon the way Jesus fulfilled the Old Testament prophecies concerning the coming of the Messiah-God

The above are just a few of the hundreds of prophecies to be found in the Old Testament concerning the coming of the Messiah-God and I have only quoted a few so that you will see that there is much more evidence for the belief that Jesus is God manifest in the flesh than you might previously have thought.

Some argue that Jesus, being familiar with the prophecies concerning the coming Messiah, might have put Himself in situations which would cause the prophecies to be fulfilled in Him.

Think of that argument for a moment and consider the conjunction of the stars at His birth—He couldn't have organised *that* could He? He couldn't have decided upon the *family* into which He would be born nor the *place* He would be born. He could not have organised that Caesar would cause 'all the world' to be taxed, thus ensuring He was born in Bethlehem, nor that Herod would slaughter the innocents and force His family to go into Egypt.

Though it is conceivable that He could have behaved in such a way as to make it probable that He would be crucified that does not explain how the prophecy regarding His crucifixion came to be written in detail many hundreds of years before crucifixion became a method of punishment in Palestine. Obviously He could not have arranged for the Romans to introduce crucifixion into Palestine!

It is improbable, though not impossible, for Jesus to have arranged for his 'own familiar friend' to betray Him but it *was* altogether impossible for Him to arrange for the priests to give Judas the thirty pieces of silver, to arrange that Judas would throw them down in the house of the Lord or to ensure that the priests would purchase the potter's field with the money.

The ancient prophets predicted what the Roman soldiers would say and do at the foot of the cross. It was predicted that they would cast lots for His vestment, revile Him, say 'If you are the son of God, save yourself' and *not* break His legs. All those prophecies were fulfilled to the letter at the crucifixion of Jesus. There is no way in which Jesus could have influenced those things.

I think it is inevitable that any unbiased thinking person who peruses the prophecies of the Old Testament regarding the Messiah-God must conclude that *'truly this was the Son of God'*.

12 *God the Father, Son and Holy Spirit*

Ｏne of the Christian concepts with which some new Christians have difficulty is that of the Holy Trinity.

Christianity being a *revealed religion* it is essential, as with *all* doctrines of the Christian faith, to precede any study with a request, directed to the Holy Spirit, that He will shed enlightenment on the subject and guide us into all truth.

Jesus said:

> If you love me, keep my commandments. And I will pray the Father and he shall give you another Comforter, that he may abide with you for ever; even the Spirit of truth, *whom the world cannot receive, because it seeth him not,* neither knoweth him; for he dwelleth *with* you and shall be *in* you.
>
> John 14:15–17

GOD THE FATHER, SON AND HOLY SPIRIT

Jesus was, of course, speaking while He was on earth and before the outpouring of the Holy Spirit on the Day of Pentecost. Though the Holy Spirit was at that time *with* His disciples, they had not as yet had the experience of having the Holy Spirit *in* them.

Let us again note that the truth which the Holy Spirit was to show the disciples was something *'the world cannot receive'*.

Unless we call upon the Holy Spirit to guide us in all things we shall resort to human reasoning and fall into the trap we are warned of in the Scriptures when it says:

> Keep that which is committed to thy trust, avoid profane and vain babblings, and oppositions of knowledge falsely so called, which some, professing, have erred concerning the faith.
> 1 Timothy 6:20–21

One God or three Gods?

The Bible tells us that there is *one* God:

> Hear, O Israel: The Lord our God is one Lord.
> Deuteronomy 6:4

Yet in another place the Bible tells us:

> For there are three that bear record in heaven, the Father, the Word, and the Holy Spirit; and these three are one.   1 John 5:7

The teaching of the triune aspect of the Godhead can be seen demonstrated throughout the New Testament. The record of the baptism of Jesus is one example:

> And Jesus, when he was baptized, went up straightway out of the water; and, lo, the heavens were opened unto him, and he saw *the Spirit of God* descending like a dove and lighting upon him.
>
> And, lo, *a voice from heaven,* saying, This is my beloved Son, in whom I am well pleased.
>
> Matthew 3:16–17

We have in that scripture three manifestations of God. There is the subject of the baptism, Jesus. Then there is the Holy Spirit descending from heaven as a dove and thirdly the voice of God the Father speaking from heaven.

We have read also the statement of Jesus to His disciples:

> And I *[the Son]* will pray the Father *[the Father]*, and he shall give you another Comforter *[the Holy Spirit]*, that he may abide with you for ever; even the Spirit of truth, whom the world cannot receive.
>
> John 14:16–17

Here again we have the three: Jesus who makes the request, the Father who will receive the request and the Comforter who will be sent in answer to the request.

There are several things about those scriptures which may well mystify the new Christian. How, for example, can God be *one God* and yet three persons who are equally God? How can Jesus be God when, as in the baptismal incident, the voice of God is heard from heaven while Jesus was being baptised?

God manifest in the flesh

Here we will have to refresh our memories yet again about the nature of God. We have seen that God is a Spirit and that He does not therefore respond to the human senses of hearing, touch, taste, smell or vision.

How then can the invisible God make Himself known to His creation? One way, as we have seen, is for Him to provide a 'sixth sense', *the faith factor*.

Another way God was able to make Himself known was to manifest Himself in various ways audibly and visually. Throughout the Old Testament God did this in a variety of ways and each illustrated an aspect of His existence.

The ultimate manifestation of God came when God took on Himself human nature and walked the earth in a human body.

We are told that in Jesus God had divested Himself of all His glory (Hebrews 2:9) and all His power and thus, while on earth, Jesus was an ordinary human being who had extraordinary powers only when they were given Him from on high.

Jesus even had the same feelings and temptations that we have (Hebrews 4:15). It was no fake or qualified humanity with which God clothed Himself but a body the same in every respect as our mortal bodies.

Jesus was *God manifest in the flesh* and we have seen that a manifestation is there to show us something we would not otherwise be able to see and teach us something we would not otherwise be able to learn.

Everything Jesus said and did He did to teach us something about God—He *was* God manifesting Himself to us in the flesh. What He did He did for *effect* and what He said He said for *effect*.

When Jesus was on earth God was manifesting Himself in a human body as *the Son of God* and Jesus behaved as the Son of God and spoke as the Son of God.

That much would present no difficulty but the fact that Jesus was able to reveal God to man did nothing to make sinful man more acceptable to God. We must therefore recognise two of the main functions Jesus came to perform: (1) To reveal God to man and (2) To represent sinful man before the throne of a holy God. The first function was that of a prophet and the second function that of the Great High Priest (Hebrews 5:6). In addition to those two functions He came also as the sacrificial offering that would take away the sins of the world (John 1:29).

Jesus exercised the dual role of the traditional prophet. He not only preached the message that God wanted humanity to hear but also foretold events which were future to His time.

As the Great High Priest He made, and still makes, intercession for our sins for the Bible says, 'There is *one* mediator between God and man, the man Christ Jesus' (1 Timothy 2:5). As the Lamb of God He died a sacrificial death on the altar of the cross, just as many a sacrificial lamb had died before Him, except that *His* sacrifice was a once-and-for-all sacrifice, to be brought once and for all before God (Hebrews 9:24–26).

The many colours of refracted light

So whenever, when He was on earth, Jesus spoke of God the Great Spirit as 'Father' He was showing forth the child/father relationship which exists between all who are born of God and their heavenly Father. He was speaking within the confines of His manifestation and with the imagery that that manifestation demanded.

I have a crystal glass paperweight which I use more as an ornament than for any practical purpose. Looked at in a certain way it is absolutely clear glass without any hint of colour. When the light shines from various angles it refracts the light into the various colours of the spectrum and takes on different colours depending on how I look at it.

We may think of that paperweight as being illustrative of the many facets of truth Jesus came to portray. If you asked a number of people who had seen it in different lights what colour my paperweight is they would give different answers: some would say green, some blue and yet others red. They would not be contradicting each other, there would be no need to prove one of them right and the others wrong. What they would actually be seeing is *the manifestation of the moment*.

The various facets of the character of God refracted through Jesus may sometimes, to the human mind, make His sayings and claims seem contradictory.

When, for example, Jesus cried when He was on the cross 'My God, my God, why hast thou forsaken me' He was showing forth one facet of Divine truth, that is, that God cannot tolerate sin—God always rejects sin. Jesus need not have said it! Jesus could communicate with God without using human speech. Anyway the question was, from His point of view, superfluous. He knew why God had forsaken the humanity with which He had clothed Himself—He was bearing our sins in His own body on the tree (1 Peter 2:24). If Jesus had not said it though—*we would not have known it!*

A rather weak but helpful illustration is that of an actor in a film. He knows the end from the beginning because he has read the script but he still goes through the whole performance as though *he did not know* that he was to fall over a cliff at the end of it. Why does he do that? Because if he didn't do it he would not be able to reveal to us the story. From the beginning of the film we are being introduced to the various characters and the circumstances which surround them. We are given glimpses of the relationship of the characters to one another and of the things which have brought about the conflict between them.

The actor says 'Will you marry me Charlotte?'—he *knows* Charlotte will marry him, he's read it in the script but if he didn't speak his line *how are we going to know* the story? The actor is *manifesting* the story to us.

Apart from the functional aspects of Jesus' life on earth I must return once again to the great gulf which exists between the things human intelligence is capable of understanding and the imponderable wonders of the spiritual world. For now we see through a glass darkly!

Many things seem to be mysteries to us because we have no words to describe them and there is nothing within our experience to which we can liken them.

The illustrations I shall give in this chapter are not held out to be anything other than a means by which the finite mind can appreciate something about that doctrine which the Christian church calls the doctrine of *the Trinity*.

I have mentioned before that any simile we may use, even the parables that Jesus used, if pressed beyond the point they were intended to illustrate can lead to false doctrine and unnecessary dogma. I do not claim that anything I say in this chapter accurately describes either the function or nature of *the Trinity* but I hope it will lead

GOD THE FATHER, SON AND HOLY SPIRIT

to some kind of understanding or something which must, of necessity, remain a mystery.

Much of the difficulty regarding the understanding of the Holy Trinity has more to do with the inadequacy of words than with any real difficulty.

What precisely is a 'person'?

The main problem the concept of the 'Trinity' presents to most people is that they cannot understand how one person can be *three* different people, or persons, or how *three* persons can be *one* person. The problem is brought about because, as we have seen, we know almost nothing about the nature of a spirit or how it exists nor do we take a great deal of time to define the word 'person'.

Can we think of a spirit as being a 'person' in the generally accepted sense of the word? Well what *is* the generally accepted sense of the word? The *Oxford Illustrated Dictionary* defines the word 'person' as it applies to God as 'Each of three distinctions or modes of divine being, in the Godhead, God the Father, Son, Holy Ghost.'

We must not confuse the word 'person' as applied to God with the same word when we think of a human being. It is not a word, by the way, which the Bible itself ever applies to God.

At the bottom of all the confusion regarding the Holy Trinity is this word 'person' as applied to Father, Son and Holy Ghost. It is the word 'person' that causes us to begin to think of the Great Universal Spirit in physical terms.

We can understand why painters of religious pictures and workers in religious art felt the need to portray God in human terms and we must respect the fact that they in sincerity performed an act of worship through their talents, but I must repeat that one of the ten commandments is *'thou shalt make unto thyself no graven image nor any likeness of any thing that is in heaven above or in earth beneath.'* Notice that the commandment is not that thou shalt not 'worship' but that 'thou shalt not *make*.'

As we have seen, the reason for that commandment is that if we make something which we purport to be a likeness of God then those who see that likeness will think of God in that way and find themselves unable to appreciate that God has no human form. Thus there has grown up a vision of God as a rather old man with a long beard who sits on a throne supported by a white cloud.

The devil is often portrayed as a half-human being with a long tail, cloven hooves, horns and a trident in his hand. This, of course, does nothing to help us believe in that very important entity, the supreme evil spirit which the Bible calls the 'devil' and 'Satan'. The devil, as is God, is a spirit and is without human form. Just as 'no man hath seen God at any time' so no man has seen the devil at any time though many have seen and experienced manifestation of that spirit.

God has no body other than the body in which He chose to *manifest* Himself. So forget, if you can, the God of the religious art. Release yourself from the idea that God looks like a human being, then, and only then, will you appreciate that the Trinity is not at all an impossibility.

It is very easy to speak of 'Three persons in one Godhead' but less easy, in this context, to define precisely what we mean by the word 'persons'.

Put this concept before someone who has seen various depictions of God in religious art and effigy and he finds it altogether impossible to appreciate three people 'persons' each with two arms, two legs, two ears, etc, existing in one 'person' who also has two arms, two legs, two ears, etc. In his mind, though he may not literalise the image, he continues to see God the Father as an old man sitting on that throne somewhere in the heavens and God the Son as a younger man sitting on a throne at His side—he will probably have a less clear idea of how the Holy Spirit should look.

Inevitably difficulties arise when our view of God is of a human kind of person with definable physique. Difficulties tend to disappear, however, immediately we grasp the concept that God is a Spirit and does not exist, except as manifest in Jesus, in any physical form. Only then can we grasp that the form of His existence is not confined within any physical or material limitation.

We may well read again what the Bible says about what men have done to the image of God:

> Professing themselves to be wise, they became fools, and changed the glory of the incorruptible God into an image made like corruptible man, and to birds, and four-footed beasts, and creeping things. Romans 1:22–23

This materialistic image-making—and I do not imply idolatry—is at the very heart of the problem. I intend no 'sideswipe' at any branch of the Christian church when I say that. It makes no difference whether the image is of wood or stone or merely a printed image on a gospel tract, the same applies. Image-making is something of which most of us are guilty at some time or other even if it is only private image-making in our own mind. It is *always* damaging to our true perception of God because we invariably find ourselves imagining God as 'solid matter'.

Immediately we begin to ask ourselves precisely what we mean by the word 'person' then the clouds of mystery begin to clear somewhat. Obviously we do not mean 'person' in the sense we apply that word to a human being.

Do you mean perhaps three separate manifestations and functions?

Let us consider Joe Bloggs

Joe Bloggs is a rather ordinary chap yet he exists in many manifestations and many functions. Joe Bloggs is the father of his daughter, the son of his mother, the husband of his wife and the brother of his brother. Joe Bloggs is also a motorist sometimes, a pedestrian sometimes and a pilot (of a microlight aircraft) sometimes.

So why do we call Joe Bloggs father, son, husband and brother? If he is one person then why do we not just regard him as being one person and have done with it? Why do we speak of him with different names at different times?

The answer of course is obvious—though Joe Bloggs is a pedestrian at times, it would be ridiculous, if he was driving his car and was stopped for speeding, for the policeman to tell the court a pedestrian had been stopped doing 90 miles an hour down the motorway. Though Joe Bloggs *is* a pedestrian—his function or manifestation at the time of the speeding offence was that of driver and motorist.

Joe Blogg's relationship to his daughter, his mother, his wife and his brother are entirely different and he will behave differently in each function. But Joe Bloggs is

GOD THE FATHER, SON AND HOLY SPIRIT

not four 'persons'. Then are we saying that Joe Bloggs the father is not a person? Is not Joe Bloggs the son a person? Is not Joe Bloggs the husband a person? Is not Joe Bloggs the brother a person? Yes indeed in each of these aspects Joe Bloggs is a person and at one and the same time both the same and a different person!

Joe Bloggs is unfortunate: he is staying at his mother's house for the weekend when the house burns down. Joe Bloggs is badly burnt—the newspaper headline reads 'Son injured in house blaze.'

His daughter is getting married but Joe breaks his leg the morning of the wedding while he is putting the cat out. The newspaper headline reads 'Father breaks leg putting cat out.'

Both headlines are accurate and if you transposed the words 'son' and 'father' from one to the other would become ridiculous. Both 'Joe Bloggs' are the *same person* but in different *manifestations* or functions.

You see the problem with us trying to understand the mystery of the Godhead is one of semantics—words. We have not got words with which we can accurately describe that which is spiritual and that which is spirit, yet some would try to define the Godhead as though we have the accuracy of expression in spiritual things that one would demand in an exact science.

Viewed in the light of what we have said about our fictional character Joe Bloggs we should have little difficulty appreciating why Jesus sometimes spoke to God the Father in His manifestation as God the Son, yet at other times spoke *as* God the Father.

Immediately we stop thinking of God being three persons, each one with arms, legs and a head; once we stop thinking of God, except for His fleshly manifestation in Jesus, as being flesh, blood and bone, or any other form of solid matter, we will find no difficulty in appreciating the individual personalities of each of the manifestations or functions of the one God—Father, Son and Holy Spirit.

Try this experiment

Now think of the three 'persons' in the Godhead as *three different manifestations* of one God rather than three different people.

Take a large bowl of ordinary tap water.

Heat that water until it boils and you will see that, without adding anything to it or taking anything away from it, it becomes steam.

Now catch that steam on a cold surface and it will turn to water again.

Take that water and put it into your deepfreeze and the water will turn to ice and then heat it again and, depending on how much you heat it, it will turn to either water or steam.

Take three small bowls and divide the water between them; freeze one bowl to make ice, boil one bowl to create steam and leave one bowl as water.

Cause the steam to condense and run back into one bowl, cause the ice to melt in the other bowl and, together with the bowl in which the water has not changed from water, pour them back into the big bowl.

Now recognising that you are only dealing with one element—water—try a few experiments with words. Let us take one extreme stance and say that it doesn't matter what you call water at any given time because, whatever its form, it really is water all the time.

So let's follow that line of thought through! It's a hot summer's day and you have a drink in your hand—ask someone to put some steam in it! You obviously want ice but it really doesn't matter because it's the same thing isn't it?

You drive to work one winter's morning and your car skids on the ice and hits another car. You tell the other motorist that you skidded on a patch of steam—but it doesn't matter because steam, ice and water are all the same thing really!

It's a cold winter's night. Are you going to ask someone to put ice in your hot water bottle?

That is why, though there is one God, and only one God, we should not be careless when we speak of God the Father, God the Son and God the Holy Spirit. Each person—and now you should know what we mean by that word and what we do not mean by that word—manifestation or, if you like, function of the Godhead is individual.

We have seen throughout this book that human reason is inadequate for understanding the things of God and so I would emphasise again that the above illustrations *are* only illustrations—they are not intended to modify the generally accepted theology of orthodox trinitarian teaching. We, as always and in all things, must rely on *revelation* through the Holy Spirit and the Scriptures, 'For there are three that bear record in heaven, the Father, the Word, and the Holy Spirit; and these three are one' (1 John 5:7).

However one wishes to express the fact, there can be no doubt that the Scriptures speak of God the Father, Son and Holy Spirit!

13 *Creation or Evolution?*

IN 1859 CHARLES DARWIN published his derivative work *The Origin of Species* and, unintentionally, caused millions of people to assume that there was henceforth no need to believe in a creator.

Darwin, as we have seen, did not in *The Origin of Species* deny the existence of a creator though he did deny the then basis of the church's teaching about the way in which the world had come into being.

Unfortunately overliteralisation by some Christians had made the church vulnerable. There was no room in fundamentalist thinking for the concept that the creation story is one of God's word pictures and one of God's great simplifications which was designed to help ordinary people understand what scientists themselves *can still only guess at*.

So let us look at what the Bible *really* says on the topic of evolution/creation.

CREATION OR EVOLUTION?

Moses pre-empted Darwin by over 3,500 years!

About 1500 BC—some 3,500 years before Darwin was born—Moses gave an account of the beginning of the earth and the life which is upon it. On examination we find that that account is more up-to-date today than the theory of evolution as it was propounded by Darwin.

It is one of the hallmarks of the Divine inspiration of the Bible that Moses knew many years ago the exact details of how the earth and the life upon it came into being.

We must appreciate that, at the time he wrote, Moses' knowledge was quite unique. At the time, among the ancients, there were many weird and fantastic theories about how things began. This *one man*, one man of all the men of his time, was correct in what he wrote about the origin of things. He told the complete story and it is only now *that science is catching up with him!*

Doubts are being cast on the theory of evolution as it used to be taught. It is now generally acknowledged that the gradual evolution of man from a lower form of life cannot be accepted as the whole explanation. Scientists are coming to believe increasingly in *'the great leap forward'* theory though they are still at a loss to explain the origin of the genetic impulse which caused 'the great leap' to take place.

It is not the purpose of this book to discuss, in any detail, the theory of evolution as related to the Christian view of creation. However, there is little point in denying that the teaching of evolution in our schools and places of learning has caused some doubt in the minds of many regarding the Genesis account of creation and, as a corollary of that doubt, to doubt the very existence of the creator. Therefore, it is of importance to show that the Bible is accurate in what it teaches about how things began.

Some ancient beliefs as to how the world came into being

Almost every ethnological group has its own creation story and very fanciful many of them are!

The pre-Darwin teaching of the church was, though not quite as ridiculous as some theories, untenable enough to be demolished in a relatively short time as science began to produce evidence that the earth had not been in existence for a mere 6,000 years and had certainly not been created in 6 literal days.

Now there is nothing shameful about the church having been wrong in its interpretation of the early chapters of Genesis for the church does not, or should not, claim infallibility. Apart from which we are after all, though Christians, still people of our time who 'see through a glass darkly' and unfortunately have the glass tinted with the tints of our time.

Still at no time was Christian thought anywhere nearly as ridiculous as non-Christian theories of how the world began.

Among the *Crow Indians* it was believed that long ago there existed only water on which swam ducks. The sun, which they conceived of as being the creator, became merged with the transformer known as the 'Coyote' and told the ducks to dive into the waters. From the mud attached to the webbed feet of the ducks he created the earth and caused it to be inhabited by living creatures.

An *Egyptian* creation story tells of everything being created from the dry land which appeared out of the 'abysmal ocean'. Amon, god of the sun and father of all the other gods, also came from the abyss. One legend has it that he appeared as a child sitting in the centre of a lotus bud.

Babylonian creation myth had it that Marduk, the god of Babylon, made the earth from the two parts of the body of Tiamat, a chaos dragon. Marduk is said to have destroyed Tiamat after a protracted battle.

Hinduism postulated a universe of immense proportions—in which view, it was, of course, correct. It conceived the 'Day of Brahma' as being the fundamental cosmic cycle, a cycle which they thought would last for some 4,320,000,000 years.

At the beginning of the Day of Brahma Vishnu is said to have lain asleep upon the cobra Shesha who floated upon the cosmic ocean, the primeval chaos. From Vishnu's navel grew a lotus, from the bud of which was born the god Brahma, who in turn created the universe on behalf of Vishnu. Vishnu then awoke and controlled the cosmos during 4,520,000,000 years of its existence.

Shaktas believed that a mother goddess gave birth to the universe after an act of sexual intercourse with her husband Shiva!

Norse legends have as the prime mover a giant 'Ymir' who created a six-headed giant by rubbing his feet together and thus producing a son and a daughter who, they believed, appeared from under his armpit. The god Odin and his two brothers killed Ymir and created the world from his body, the earth from his flesh, the mountains from his bones, the sky from his skull and the sea from his blood.

Such were the ancient views of creation and it is against that background of fanciful theories that we should look at the creation story of the prophet Moses and wonder at the scientific accuracy we find in it.

The conflict between the theory of evolution and the doctrine of creation

I have always found it difficult to understand why there should be a conflict between the concept of evolution and the doctrine of creation—the terms are not in themselves opposites.

There are two ladies with whom I am acquainted who, though otherwise quite unexceptional, had the extraordinary ability to talk to each other, each talking on a different subject. One would happily talk about the price of groceries while the other would talk about her holidays. They were quite oblivious to the fact that they were not talking about the same thing but it seemed to be, to them, a satisfactory and satisfying arrangement.

Those ladies are only a little more odd than some of the protagonists in the evolution versus creation debate who seem not to realise they are talking about two different subjects. Some Darwinians still argue the case for evolution as though the doctrine of creation is an affront to that theory, whilst many creationists argue against the theory of evolution, root and branch, as though 'evolution' is the opposite to 'creation'—which it is not.

Charles Darwin, as we have seen, believed in a 'creator' and therefore in 'creation' and, it will come as a surprise to some to learn, the prophet Moses proposed a theory of evolution 3,500 years before Darwin was born.

The *Oxford Dictionary* defines the word evolution as, among other meanings, 'Development, detailed working out of what is implicitly or potentially contained in an idea or principle; development from rudimentary to mature or complete state. Origination of species of animals and plants by process of development from earlier forms.' If one reads the first chapter of Genesis it becomes obvious that in the 'days' of creation God developed the earth 'from a rudimentary to a mature or complete state'.

To everyone with preconceived ideas—and haven't we all got some preconceived ideas?—I would say: read what Darwin really taught, read what Moses really taught, bring yourself up to date with present-day scientific thinking and you will discover that Moses had the most inspired piece of insight into the beginning of life on our planet in history!

Do not, I appeal to you, defend *what you think Moses wrote;* read what he *did* write and believe what he did write, not what you have always been taught to believe he wrote.

It is futile for any of us to try and gainsay, and we should not want to gainsay, many of the facts which modern discovery has brought before us. It is equally futile for scientists to pretend that any one of their many hypotheses are certain knowledge. There is indeed a kernel of truth in the snide remark of the fellow who was asked what he thought of current scientific opinion and replied, 'I don't know—I haven't read today's newspapers!'

Yes, science *has* had its quiverful of 'certainties' since Darwin but one by one they have been replaced by new ideas and superseded because new discoveries proved them not to be the certainties they were thought to be.

The miracle some men of religion missed

The history of misinterpretation of the Scriptures is the history of preconceived ideas being allowed to take preeminence over fact. Because it is human for us to become enmeshed in our own preconceived ideas, it is easy to miss the real wonder of the Biblical creation story, a wonder which stamps the Genesis story as being inspired of God.

Only an authority beyond human authority *could reveal the exact sequence of the coming into being of the earth and the life upon it 3,500 years before the world heard the name Darwin.*

In only one vital respect does Moses' account differ from the conclusions of Darwin—it explained, which Darwin could not explain, and science has still not explained, a phenomenon which science even today has to call 'the missing link'. Only now, 125 years after Darwin, is science beginning to get it right!

In the beginning

Let us compare what Moses wrote with the facts as more and more scientists are beginning to see them:

> In the beginning God created the heaven and the earth. And the earth was without form and void.
> Genesis 1:1

I want you to notice the word 'was', for literally translated from the Hebrew the word is 'became'. There is therefore in the original text a distinct statement that the earth was in existence before it 'became' without form and void.

It is worthy of note too that there is no statement as to how long, before the earth *became* without form and void, it had been in existence. There is sufficient latitude in those unexplored eras of earth's pre-history to take into account the many facts of science which show our earth to be millions of years old.

CREATION OR EVOLUTION?

The earth was without form and void

The earth was without form and void.

A most unusual phrase to use, for what element is 'without form and void'?

The only element that can truly be said to be without form and void is—*gas!* Is it not surprising that it is only in recent years that science has come to the conclusion that our earth was originally a cloud of gas which later solidified?

How would Moses have known that if he was not inspired of God?

The 'six days' of creation

Much has been made by critics of Moses' assertion that the world was made in 'six days'. Atheists have scoffed at it and some believers have become hot under the collar defending the concept. Some literalists have felt it necessary, in all sincerity, to insist that the world was created in six literal 'days'.

The word translated 'day' is the Hebrew word *yom* and is variously translated 'day', 'time', 'age' and 'season'—it is certainly not necessary to insist upon it indicating a twenty-four-hour day.

More than sixty-five times the prophets Zephaniah, Isaiah, Zechariah and Joel refer to a period of time they call 'The *day* of the Lord'—now I think the most fundamentalist Christian will recognise that 'The day of the Lord' is not one single twenty-four-hour day but rather a period of time. The word translated 'day' in 'The *day* of the Lord' is the same word *yom* we find translated 'day' in Genesis.

The six days of Genesis are periods of time and no indication is given as to how long those periods of time lasted. It is entirely irrelevant to the Christian gospel whether they were six thousand years, six million years or six billion years in length!

The first stage of creation

Science has it that gradually this great cloud of gas solidified and that during the solidification period the atmosphere was so dense that no light penetrated to the earth's surface.

The 'first day' or 'period' is one of the most controversial periods of the creation story as written by Moses. His words 'And God said, let there be light: and there was light' have been the centre of many a controversy.

Yet the body of scientific opinion has now come to the conclusion that that is what actually happened! In the first period of earth's existence the gas solidified, the atmosphere thinned and the earth became light—rather as a sea fog lifting in early morning and letting the sun shine on the sea.

It is often pointed out by those who are more critical than understanding, that the sun, moon and stars are not said by Moses to have been created until the fourth 'day' and yet light is said to have appeared on the first 'day'.

Moses was not so naive a person that he was unaware that he had written of there being light before he had mentioned the existence of the sun, moon and stars. Moses was an intelligent man brought up in the royal household of Egypt and conversant with the skills of astronomy and astrology. He could easily have written that the sun, moon and stars appeared in the heavens on the first 'day' but had he done so he would have been scientifically wrong. He was aware, as we are aware, that the earth's light comes from the sun and moon and a very little from the stars. Then why did he write that light appeared *before* the sun, moon and stars?

Think of the sea mist I have mentioned. It is night and visibility is as little as twenty feet. Dawn breaks and it becomes light but it is still not possible to see the sun or the moon—it is not until the fog disperses, and that may take days or weeks, that one is able to see the sun and moon.

That is precisely what science agrees happened—the earth became light *before* the vapours had cleared enough for the sun, moon and stars to be seen from the surface of the earth.

It would have been easy, and in keeping with deduction from human observation, to have said that the sun appeared before the light—it must have seemed quite ridiculous to Moses from a human point of view that the light appeared before the sun. Yet with the complete honesty of one receiving a revelation from an outside source Moses left in the narrative something he undoubtedly did not understand.

The second stage of creation

It is accepted today that during the early millions of years of earth's existence, and after it had solidified, the earth was covered in vapour. The whole of the earth's surface was dank, wet swampland. We are told that there was no rainfall at that time. That is the modern scientific view. Now let us see what Moses said of that period of earth's history:

> For God had not caused it to rain upon the earth,

and there was not a man to till the ground. But there went up a mist from the earth, and watered the whole face of the ground. Genesis 2:5,6

Would not the evidence of Moses' eyes and mere human reason have indicated to him that the earth had always been as he had seen it during his long lifetime? How did he reach conclusions which science would not reach for another 3,500 years? From whence came his inspiration if not from God?

What is the next step in earth's development (evolution) according to present scientific opinion? It is that gradually the mists cleared from the earth's surface and the clouds formed in the heavens. In this period the earth began to receive its first rainfall. At this time too the system of evaporation to dry the earth, and condensation to form the rain came into being.

What is the Moses' account of what happened?

And God said, Let there be a firmament in the midst of the waters...And God made the firmament, and divided the waters which were *under* the firmament from the waters which were *above* the firmament. Genesis 1:6,7

The third stage of creation

It is generally believed among scientists that the next stage in the evolution of the earth came about when the general swamp, which was the earth at the time, began to separate into land masses and oceans.

What did Moses say about this period?

And God said, Let the waters under the heaven be

CREATION OR EVOLUTION?

gathered together in one place, and let the dry land appear: and it was so. And God called the dry land Earth; and the gathering together of the waters called he Seas. Genesis 1:9,10

Science agrees too that the next form of life to appear was vegetation. Moses says:

And God said, Let the earth bring forth vegetation, the herb yielding seed, and the fruit tree yielding fruit of its kind, whose seed is in itself, upon the earth; and it was so. Genesis 1:11

The fourth stage of creation

Scientists tell us that it was at this time that the clouds which had girdled the earth in a seamless garment of vapour began to break up and there were periods when the skies were clear. For the first time, had there been life on earth with eyes to behold them, the sun, moon and stars would have become visible.

What does Moses say about this period?

And God said, Let there be lights in the firmament of the heaven to divide the day from the night; and let them be for signs, and for seasons, and for days, and years. Genesis 1:14

The controversial fifth day of creation

This is the point at which the religious thought of his day and the hypothesis of Charles Darwin came into bitter and direct conflict.

Darwin taught that *all* animal life originated from

lower forms of life which had first begun in the waters on the earth's surface. Both Moses and Darwin agreed that vegetation and plants were the first forms of life on earth but Darwin went further, much further: he taught that the first living things, single cell life forms, the first animal life on earth, developed in the waters.

Later, he taught, simple life forms developed into higher forms of life: jelly fish, sea anemones, corals, comb jellies, flat worms and nemertine worms. Then came the cartilaginous fish and the bony fish such as lung fish and sturgeon, followed by the amphibians, reptiles, birds and mammals.

Darwin was laughed to scorn, not only by religious activists but also by the majority of his fellow scientists. Indeed his fellow scientists were often in the forefront of the bitter attacks upon him.

Had Darwin gone no further than to propose that *fish* had a common ancestry in the waters of the world then perhaps he would not have met with such bitter opposition, but how could anyone with common sense imagine that birds and mammals actually originated in the water?

No scientist, let alone any good sane fundamentalist Christian, could possibly comprehend, or even tolerate, the proposal that the monkey, lion, ostrich, goat, sheep or, for that matter, the dinosaur, had originated in some murky pool.

Now you have to admit that, had you not been taught it in school, it would be difficult to envisage that the ancestors of your pet cat and dog originated in a swamp—but *that* is what Darwin taught! Of course you wouldn't guess it by looking at Tibs and Bonzo would you?

Darwin and others did a lot of in-depth investigation before they convinced themselves that the theory which

CREATION OR EVOLUTION? 229

they were about to declare to the world was supportable. Darwin was not unaware that his scientific reputation was at stake.

If we rely on common observation and common sense then we must realise that birds do not come out of the water, they are born in nests! Observation certainly does not lead us to the conclusion that *all* animals and *every* living thing originated in the waters of the world!

Yet you know, had Moses been alive at the time Darwin published his theory, he would have been among the first to shake Darwin by the hand and tell him, in that respect, how right he was. Perhaps Moses would also have chided Darwin on how long it had taken him to reach that conclusion and said, 'I told you so!' Indeed Moses *had* told all of us so, 3,500 years ago:

> And God said, Let the *waters* bring forth abundantly the moving creatures that hath life, *and fowl* that may fly above the earth in the open firmament of heaven. And God created great sea monsters, and *every living creature* that moveth, *which the waters brought forth abundantly,* after their kind.
> Genesis 1:20,21

Again I say, except by Divine inspiration, how could Moses have possibly known that which his contemporaries did not know and which it has taken science 3,500 years to find out?

The sixth day of creation

It is at this point, the arrival of mankind on earth, that Moses and Darwin diverge—*but it was Darwin that got it wrong!*

Darwin taught that man was no more than an evolutionary progression from the highest form of animal. He was never, however, able to explain—and to be fair to him, Darwin readily admitted that he could not explain—the gulf which so obviously exists between the lowest form of man and the highest form of animal.

When science so desires, it can be quite as dishonest as the most bigoted among any other group of people. Science could not explain why there was an unbridged chasm between the highest form of animal and the lowest form of man when, according to the theory of evolution, the 'link' should have existed. Indeed there should not have been *one* link but millions of links in both fossil and living form.

No such 'link' was ever found—nothing that was not either wholly man or wholly animal.

I will not belabour scientists with the cruel 'Piltdown Man' hoax but it is fairly typical of the readiness of the evolutionist to grasp at straws in a desperate attempt to explain something which is completely inexplicable unless we accept the 'Great Leap' theory or Moses' account of events. Science slid carefully, disgracefully and intellectually deceitfully behind a phrase which they thought hid their lack of knowledge—'The Missing Link' was born.

If Darwin was wrong, however, so were his opponents who contended that man had had no existence at all until God said, 'Let us make man in our image.'

Darwin was wrong, his opponents were wrong, but Moses was right:

> And the Lord formed man of the dust of the ground [step one] and breathed into his nostrils the

breath of life, and [step two] man became a *living soul*. Genesis 2:7

The progression is absolutely scientific, though it has only been considered so for a very few years:

1. God created that element the Bible calls 'the dust of the ground'.
2. God formed man from that element which was by that time already in existence.
3. God caused something to happen to that creation—He breathed the breath of life into it and it *became* a living soul.

Darwin looked for a 'missing link'—it was not there! Modern scientists look for a 'great leap forward' in the development of man and Moses tells us how that *great leap forward* took place. God breathed the breath of life into man *and man became a living soul*.

Moses taught, as Darwin taught, that man was developed, evolved *and* created from elements which already existed. What elements? It matters not! What really matters is that man is not *just* a progression in evolution—he is a special creation of God. The real point is what happened to man as a result of him becoming a 'living soul'. No one can argue against the proposition that between man and animal, however, whenever or wherever it happened—there is a great gulf fixed!

No animal has a 'spiritual consciousness' such as man has, a consciousness which causes man, however primitive he be, to contemplate life after death and other spiritual issues.

That something happened to man that did not happen to animal is beyond doubt. Evolutionists may call it a 'great leap forward' genetically motivated—that puts a name to the phenomenon but does not explain it. Evolution may explain to a great degree *what happened* but the Bible explains *what caused it to happen*.

Evolution or creation?

Both! It is a non-question! They are not *alternatives*.

Let us contemplate for a moment an artist painting a picture. On day one he prepares the canvas—he has taken the first step in the evolution of the painting. Weeks pass and he paints a little of the background—he has taken another step in the evolution of the painting. Day by day, week by week, month by month the painter adds detail to the painting and it gradually evolves into a work of art.

The painting has *evolved* from being a blank canvas to being a painting: it has gone through many intermediate stages of development—it didn't all happen in a second! Does it matter how long it took for the artist to complete the painting, does it matter how little or how much he completed at each session? Perhaps the whole would take all the artist's lifetime. Does it really matter? Is the length of time or number of stages it has taken to complete the painting of the essence?

Yes, the painting *did* evolve but that is no contradiction of the fact that the artist *created* it! An act of creativity is not denominated by how long, how short or how many steps there are in the act but by the evidence of design which exists in the finished product.

Life in the world around us may well have developed and evolved but, back of that, we must recognise the life force which put within it the genetic impulse to do so.

Though the most elementary forms of life have been

produced in the laboratory by man, it has not appeared spontaneously—it has taken a great deal of intelligence on the part of man to *cause it to do so*. That is precisely what the Bible teaches; it takes a great deal of intelligence to bring order out of chaos—*in the beginning God!*

14 *The relationship between faith and behaviour*

WE HAVE READ the scripture 'For by grace are ye saved, through faith; and that not of yourselves: it is the gift of God; not of works, lest any man should boast' (Ephesians 2:8–9).

Some have taken that scripture to mean that works, the things people do and the way they behave, have no part to play in the Christian life. That is quite an untenable view and out of keeping with the whole body of Bible teaching.

The Christian life is anything but the soft option!

A parable of a postage stamp

To illustrate the relationship between grace (unmerited favour) and works (the things we do and how we behave) perhaps the following 'parable' will help.

There is before me as I write a very small piece of

paper perforated around the edges—it is a postage stamp.

It is a *British* postage stamp made thus by the sovereign will of Her Majesty the Queen.

The scrap of paper before me is inanimate, it is not in the nature of the thing for it to be able to contribute to it becoming what it is. It did not will to become a postage stamp nor *could* it make any effort to become one. Had it not been chosen by royal prerogative and designed by royal command for this purpose it may well have formed part of a sheet of paper which was destined to have another, perhaps less honourable, existence.

On my desk is another postage stamp but not a British stamp—it is German. The *imprint* upon this stamp is quite different from the imprint of the British stamp.

We continue, in our churches, to debate the relationship between salvation and works. I think the postage stamp illustrates the relationship between sovereign grace and works very well.

Just as the postage stamp was chosen to be what it is by sovereign will, so the believer is chosen to be what he or she is by sovereign will. Being, as the Bible says, 'dead in trespasses and sin', that bit of human material which eventually becomes a child of God *cannot* make the initial decision, there is nothing it can do to help itself.

The believer is the product of sovereign will: his salvation is a free gift from God who chose him, called him, revealed Himself to him, gave him the ability to discern things of God (faith), provided for the remission of his sins and for his regeneration through the new birth.

It is, unfortunately, at this point so many are liable to go wrong. 'Ah,' someone will say, 'so it *is* possible for a person to be a believer and yet there be no change in his life!' At first that may seem to be the logical conclusion to be drawn from the doctrine that a person's salvation is *all of grace and nothing of works*.

That conclusion is quite erroneous, however. What is the difference between the two postage stamps before me? Apart from the fact that the one was issued by the sovereign will of the Queen and the other by the will of the German government there is another difference. *The two bear different images!*

Though the British postage stamp did nothing, indeed could do nothing, to ensure that it became a British postage stamp, the *proof* that it *is* a British postage stamp is *in its design*. Any other design than that decreed by the sovereign and it is not a British postage stamp.

No, it is not possible for a man to be chosen of God unto salvation and remain unchanged. When God chooses a person He stamps *His* image upon them and there will be no doubt as to what that person is—any other image and the stamp is either of a different government or a fake.

Enjoying the benefits of life in the new dimension depends upon obedience

As we have seen, the salvation of God starts *now!* Christianity is no mere code of conduct which looks wholly to a future life for its rewards—in fact I would say from personal experience that if there *were* no future life, the quality of life Christianity bestows in the here-and-now is well worth having for its own sake. Freedom from the guilt of the past, peace, assurance, joy and contentment are all treasures more precious than gold!

But it stands to reason doesn't it that you will not be very happy in even an earthly relationship if you go out

THE RELATIONSHIP BETWEEN FAITH AND BEHAVIOUR 237

of your way to displease the other people who are with you in that relationship. In your relationship with your earthly father, for example, if you go out of your way to do things which are abhorrent to him then you would not expect the relationship to be good. Of course, with your earthly parents you take care not to do things which they dislike or you make sure you do them without their knowledge. There is the point too that the rules made by your earthly parents may be unfair or out of date and you feel that you have the right to live your life your own way.

Nothing that God asks of you is unreasonable and the promise you made when you accepted Jesus Christ as your own personal Saviour was that you would no longer live your life in your own way but in God's way. Furthermore, it is quite impossible to do anything which is against God's will without His knowledge.

There is an old hymn which is full of meaning:

> When we walk with the Lord
> In the light of His word,
> What glory He sheds on our way,
> While we do His good will,
> He abides with us still,
> And with all who will trust and obey.
> Trust and obey,
> For there's no other way,
> To be happy in Jesus,
> But to trust and obey.

You would not expect to have a very happy life in your social circle if you insisted on breaking the common rules of etiquette that social circle expected of you. You would soon come to grief at work if you did not behave in the way expected of you.

Similarly, the earthly benefits of life in the new dimension will only be experienced by you by obeying the rules.

Faith results in the desire to obey

The Bible says:

> This, then, is the message which we have heard of him, and declare unto you, that God is light, and in him is no darkness at all.
>
> If we say that we have fellowship with him, and walk in the darkness, *we lie, and do not the truth;*
>
> But if we walk in the light, as he is in the light, we have fellowship one with another, and the blood of Jesus Christ, his Son, cleanseth us from all sin. 1 John 1:5–7

The Bible says again:

> And by this *we do know that we know him,* if we keep his commandments.
>
> He that saith, I know him, and keepeth not his commandments, *is a liar,* and the truth is not in him.
>
> But whosoever keepeth his word, in him verily is the love of God perfected; by this know we that we are in him.
>
> He that saith he abideth in him ought himself also to walk, even as he walked. 1 John 2:3–6

Obedience to the revealed will of God—the initial evidence of the new birth

It is a matter of cause and effect! Salvation is *not* obtained as a result of the way a person lives but the way a person lives is *essential evidence* of their salvation. Make no mistake about this, whatever you may *pretend* to be, you are only God's if you have God's imprint upon you.

In that wonderful chapter John 10—everyone should read it carefully several times—Christ says, 'But ye believe not, because ye are not of my sheep, as I said unto you. My sheep hear my voice, and I know them, and they follow me' (verses 26 and 27).

Note carefully—it is very easy to transpose the order of things—Jesus did not say that they were His sheep because they heard His voice but that they heard His voice *because they were His sheep*.

There is cause and effect clearly stated in that scripture and it is never permissible to transpose cause and effect. The 'cause' of a person becoming a believer or follower of Jesus is that God has made that person His own by opening his eyes (faith) to the things which are otherwise beyond human understanding and the 'effect' is that the believer hears the voice of God and has an indwelling desire to obey it.

That is the *initial evidence* that a person has received *the faith factor*—the evidence that that person is eager to obey the will of God. That is why, in the early church, the disciples insisted on baptism in water immediately following the confession of faith. This act of obedience, an act carried out before most of the new converts had been in the church long enough to understand its implications, was evidence that they were saying in their hearts 'Where *He* leads me I will follow.'

By faith Abraham did not sit down and do nothing to help himself, *he went* into a far country and even made arrangements to sacrifice his own son. By faith Noah did not just wait for the flood to come, *he worked* to prepare an ark. By faith Moses did not wait for God to deliver the children of Israel, *he acted*. *Without* faith none of those men would have known *what they were supposed to do* but faith inspired them to action—they did things for God.

It is not difficult to print stamps—trading companies used to do it and every 'Banana Republic' on earth does it. It is not difficult to make church members, nor to get thousands of people to raise their hands in religious meetings, but the acid test comes when we look closely and see whose image those 'converts' bear.

True conversion brings with it repentance and an aversion to offending against the laws of God. I once knew an old Christian who put it this way: 'I still steal as much as I like, I still commit adultery as much as I like and I still get drunk as much as I like—but since Christ came into my heart I *don't like!*'

By their fruits you will know them

Jesus had a lot to say about trees and the fruit they bear. Note yet again as you read these words of Jesus that He does *not* contend that a tree *becomes* a good tree because it brings forth good fruit. Jesus emphasises that the fruit a tree will bring forth will depend upon the nature of that tree.

> Ye shall know them by their fruits. Do men gather grapes of thorns, or figs of thistles?

> Even so, every good tree bringeth forth good fruit, but a corrupt tree bringeth forth evil fruit.
>
> A good tree *cannot* bring forth evil fruit, neither *can* a corrupt tree bring forth good fruit.
>
> Every tree that bringeth not forth good fruit is hewn down, and cast into the fire.
>
> Wherefore by their fruits ye shall know them. Not everyone that saith unto me, Lord, Lord, shall enter into the kingdom of heaven, but he that doeth the will of my Father, who is in heaven.
>
> Many will say to me in that day, Lord, Lord, have we not prophesied in thy name? And in thy name have cast out devils? And in thy name done many wonderful works?
>
> And then I will profess unto them, *I never knew you;* depart from me, ye that work iniquity.
>
> Matthew 7:16–23

The initial and abiding evidence that Jesus has done a work of grace in our hearts is the way we behave. To think that a person can be born again of the Spirit of God and remain unchanged is a basic denial of the whole miraculous concept of the new birth.

If you go into your local garden centre and purchase an apple tree you will not expect it to produce plums. If the tree you purchase as an apple tree, the tree you take home and tend so carefully *does* produce plums then you would be in no doubt that you have been sold *the wrong tree!*

The fact that the tree produces plums will have nothing to do with the way you label it and feed it, nor its position in your garden. It will have to do with one factor and one factor only—the nature of the thing.

If *divine nature* is flowing through your being then you

will produce the fruits of one who is a partaker of Divine nature. It has nothing to do with the religious jargon you speak, the fact that you enjoy going to church, the fact that the singing of hymns moves you deeply or the *mental* assent you give to the doctrines of the church. You are either an apple tree and you will produce apples or you are not an apple tree and you will not produce apples.

If you bought a dozen fertilised chicken eggs and put them in an incubator and a dozen ducks hatched you would know at once that the eggs that had been supplied to you had been produced by ducks. The ducks would not have become ducks because they looked like ducks and behaved like ducks, they would look like ducks and behave like ducks because *they were ducks*. They would not be the children of ducks because they looked like ducks and behaved like ducks, they would look like ducks and behave like ducks because they were the children of ducks.

So the child of God does not become a child of God because of the way he lives but the way he lives will be dominated by the fact that he is a child of God.

15 *It's decision time!*

AT THE BEGINNING of this book I said that there was something very unusual happening in your life for you to want to read a book of this kind—that you have continued to read it through to the end is even more significant!

I have emphasised through that '*natural* man receiveth not the things of the Spirit of God; for they are foolishness unto him; *neither can he know them,* because they are spiritually discerned' (1 Corinthians 2:14).

Then why are *you* finding the things of God of interest? It is my belief that you have found this book of interest because the Spirit of God is calling you to join that chosen band of people for whom Christ prayed, as recorded in John chapter 17. I quote just a few words from that chapter but I think it as well if you read the whole of the chapter.

I have manifested thy name unto the men whom

thou gavest me out of the world; thine they were, and thou gavest them to me...I pray for them; I pray not for the world, but for them whom thou hast given me: for they are thine. (verses 6 and 9)

I confess to not understanding fully the workings of the sovereignty of God but whenever I read the seventeenth chapter of John it makes me feel a very special person in the sight of God.

A disastrous inclination

We have seen that, though humankind seems impelled by some genetic impulse to seek after gods and superstitions galore in an attempt to fill that great void of spiritual need left when man fell from his original status, people will not seek after the God of the Bible unless God Himself approaches them through His Spirit.

I have an atheist friend, a good, honest, upright, family man! His wife is a committed Christian and he gives her all the support in her faith of which, within the limitations of his own beliefs, he is capable.

Nevertheless we laugh a lot about the contradictions in his life—he will not walk under a ladder, he wears a gold St Christopher on a chain around his neck believing it to be a good luck charm and if he spills salt he throws some over his shoulder! He *cannot* believe in Christianity because it demands a belief in the supernatural but he *can* believe that the act of walking under a ladder can bring 'bad luck' and that a piece of gold fashioned in the imaginary likeness of a long-dead saint can ensure safe journeys!

That man is not at all unusual—he is not the only one to have his life overshadowed by superstition yet reject

Christ because he cannot accept the supernatural message which belief in Christ demands he accepts. Why do people behave in that seemingly illogical way?

Though we know little about the great battle that is being waged in the spirit world between God and that other great universal spirit which Scripture calls 'the devil' or 'Satan'—the Bible gives it but a brief mention and anyway it is beyond our comprehension—we *do* know that part of the satanic function is to cause humankind to doubt, disobey or ignore the Word of God. That is the *real* message of the Garden of Eden narrative.

There is only one threat to the universe-conquering ambitions of the supreme evil spirit the Bible calls Satan and that is the power of Jehovah God Himself.

Why do men and women reject Christianity and yet turn to strange superstitions? Because the attack of that great anti-God power Satan is not against gods in general but against the one true and living God, the God of the Bible in particular, not against belief in the supernatural in general but against belief in the kingship of Jehovah God in particular.

There is no spiritual battle being waged to stop man believing in gods of wood and stone, there is no impediment to man believing in the power of a broken mirror to bring bad luck, there is no spiritual inhibition to people believing in ghosts, poltergeists and things that go bump in the night, there is no spiritual power telling people that they should not accept that god was an astronaut, that flying saucers with little green spacemen in them throng the heavens and no influence dissuading them from believing hundreds of things about actions which are supposed to bring either good or bad luck. It is surprising how many people who laugh at our belief in the power of God are quite prepared to believe in the power of a dead rabbit's foot!

Until we realise that the whole of the anti-God spiritual strategy is dedicated to bringing the *Word of God* into disrepute and usurping the *overall* power of God we cannot understand why people who accept superstition so readily find it so difficult to accept the supernatural doctrines of the Bible.

Yes, the natural thing for *you* to have done would have been for you to have made any of the thousand-and-one excuses which people make *not* to come face to face with Jesus Christ. You didn't make those excuses and that is much more significant than you may realise.

I don't know your circumstances of course but it is self-evident that when you began to read you were seeking for something more than you had hitherto experienced. Perhaps 'the way that seemeth right unto man' had begun to seem not so right after all! I said that 'God works in mysterious ways' and He does.

The God who seeks

The Bible says that Jesus came to seek and to save that which was lost (Luke 19:10).

It is an unfortunate misconception to conceive that God is forever waiting for people and *they* then have to make their choice.

Jesus said, 'Behold, I stand at the door, and knock; if any man hear my voice, and open the door, I will come in to him, and will sup with him, and he with me' (Revelation 3:20). That is not Jesus in a passive role, it is Jesus taking the initiative and making His presence known to man. It *could* be that those vague feelings of discontent you are experiencing have nothing to do with your environment, your job, your marriage or any of the hundred-and-one other things you may attribute them to—they *could* be God knocking on the door of your heart and mind.

The Bible is very plain in its teaching that it is *always* God who makes the first approach to man, never man to God. Jesus said, 'Ye have not chosen me, but I have chosen you' (John 15:16).

In Matthew 18:12,13 Jesus speaks of the lost sheep, an animal that could no more find its way back to the fold than an unenlightened person can find his way to God. The shepherd went out to *find* the sheep, the sheep did not look for the shepherd.

Then in Matthew 22:1–14 we read the story of the wedding feast. Despite the generosity of the invitation everyone began to make excuse as to why they should not come to the feast. Finally the king issued instructions that his servants were to go into the highways and the byways and *compel them to come in.* It's a fine illustration of the way in which God sends forth His Holy Spirit to touch the hearts of those who would not otherwise come to Him and by *divine compulsion* compels them to come in.

As I have said, the first sign that God is approaching a person is often the restless feeling that person experiences, the feeling that one is missing out on something in life, the feeling that *there is more to life than this,* a vague feeling of dissatisfaction with the way things are. Have you noticed that you are beginning to feel that way?

Do *you* consider yourself to be at peace with yourself and with God? Is your life full to the brim with *joy*—no not fun—joy? Or, despite the things you have, is there a feeling of discontent pervading your life? Is there a vague feeling, a feeling that constantly nags away in the back of your mind, that you are not fulfilling your destiny as an individual, as a person? If so perhaps you will seriously consider the possibility that God is approaching *you*.

I have seen God reach out to people so often in so many different ways and in such a wide variety of circumstances that I am left in wonder at the working of His Spirit. Sometimes the people I have seen God touch have realised that He *was* reaching out to them and sometimes, tragically, they attributed their feelings of disquiet to other things.

Yes, God moves in mysterious ways! I had a friend who was a pianist with a well-known dance orchestra when the big bands were as popular as pop groups are now. Though he enjoyed the popularity his entertainment career brought him, I began to detect in him an air of increasing dissatisfaction with life—his wife mentioned to me that she had noticed it too. He was suffering from the, as yet slight, feeling that *there must be more to life than this*.

He arrived in Blackpool one night by train for a show the following day and as he walked through the booking hall of the station his vision was drawn as if by a magnet to the large station clock—it showed the time to be *one minute to midnight!*

'I stopped,' he said, 'transfixed by the hand hovering at one minute to midnight. It seemed to me I stood there for an hour though it was actually but a few seconds.

'I played in the band the following evening but the face of that clock with its hands at one minute to midnight haunted me and I remember playing more than one "duff" note.

'On the Sunday evening I went for a walk and I seemed just to follow a crowd of people going into church. I don't know the name of the church, I don't know the name of the preacher and I don't remember much about the service but I *do* remember his text, "Thou fool, this night shall thy soul be required of thee" (Luke 12:20). Well, I accepted Christ that night and I am no longer troubled by the fact that it may be *one minute to midnight* in my life because I know now that one minute past midnight is not oblivion but the start of a new day in the presence of Jesus.'

God caused *an awareness of how quickly life passes* to bring that man to Christ!

Perhaps the Spirit of God is making *you* aware of the brevity of life in some other way! Perhaps you remember how long it seemed between Christmases when you were much younger. Now the passing of time seems to have accelerated—Christmases and birthdays seemed to flash by and you have suddenly begun to realise *how quickly your life here on earth is passing*. Perhaps God is drawing *your* attention to the brevity of life!

A woman I know was very ambitious—nothing wrong with that! She thought though that when she had accumulated sufficient wealth and possessions she would be fulfilled but she wasn't.

As the years went by she found her ambition to be a never ending road, a road without a definable time of arrival or point of arrival. She reached the pinnacle of her career, a pinnacle she richly deserved to reach, a pinnacle which she reached by honest hard work and which she had thought would bring her happiness and satisfaction.

Yet there remained a void in her life which *had* to be filled. She tried for a while to fill that void with fun and social life only to find they were not a fulfilment but an addiction which craved ever more fun and social life to sustain the 'high'.

Now this true story would have had more impact if I had been able to tell you that that woman had plunged into the depths of depravity—she did not! She remained a faithful wife and a good mother and in her social round she engaged in nothing which was depraved and nothing exceptionally evil—just an attempt to keep the feeling that *there must be more to life than this* from the forefront of her mind.

You wouldn't think that God could use a station clock to make someone aware of Himself would you? Well, the case of this young lady is even more unusual—God used an article on Elvis Presley to bring *her* to a knowledge of *her* need of Him!

One day she visited the dentist. In the waiting room, bored, she flicked through a magazine and came upon an article on the life of Elvis Presley and realised that one of the greatest entertainers the world had ever seen could not find satisfaction in his own life. Despite having enough of this world's wealth and fame to be able to acquire almost any possession or experience it is possible to acquire he lived a disconsolate life. She realised that if Elvis Presley could not find satisfaction in fame, if Elvis Presley could not find satisfaction in the social round, if Elvis Presley could not find satisfaction in wealth and possessions then she had no hope at all of doing so!

She realised that she could not buy enough entertainment, fame or possessions to fill the void in her life.

Jaded, she experienced what the hymnwriter of old experienced all those years ago when he wrote:

> I tried the broken cisterns, Lord
> But, ah! the waters failed!

> E'en as I stooped to drink they fled,
> And mocked me as I wailed.

God used success to bring that woman to Himself! She is still rich and successful but she has a new perspective on life. She still has fun and a good social life, though her idea of what fun really is has changed somewhat, but now she doesn't use them as means of escape from reality. She said to me, 'The difference then and now is that *now* I am running *towards* life and lovingly embracing it—*then* I was running *away* from it!'

That woman could have considered what was happening to her as being just 'executive stress' or 'coincidence' but what a tragedy it would have been had she done so! Whatever is happening to you I would ask you to consider whether it is God reaching out towards you—God works in mysterious ways!

A man I know, as was the prodigal son, was born into money and spent all he had by the time he was thirty years of age on profligate living. One night as he returned to the filth and degradation of his cheap London dosshouse; in the words of the parable of the prodigal son, 'He came to himself' (Luke 15:17) and reviewed his past. He wended his way back to God a much wiser man. God used poverty to bring that man to Christ! He's still a poor man but he told me that he wouldn't swop the experience he now has for a million pounds!

Now is the accepted time—now is the day of salvation

I think you know by now that God is calling *you*! Don't delay responding to His call.

Though the gospel message has been preached now

for almost two thousand years it has been my experience that God approaches any individual for a fleeting time in his or her life, perhaps an hour, perhaps a day or perhaps a week and then the chance is gone for ever. I don't know why this is but it's as though, when people do not respond to the call of God, a hardness comes upon them that serves as a resistance against any further work of the Spirit.

This is illustrated by an incident in the New Testament when Paul preached the gospel message to Felix and his wife (Acts 25). Felix heard the message and the Bible tells us that he feared so greatly that his body shook with fear. At that moment the Holy Spirit was applying the Word of God to that man's heart. Felix did not make a decision, saying to Paul 'I will hear you again on this matter.' Felix *did* hear Paul again but he never came under conviction of sin again! He sent for Paul frequently but only because he thought Paul might give him money! The moment had passed!

The Bible doesn't tell us *why* Felix dismissed the matter at that moment in his life. Perhaps he was too busy at that moment with matters of state, perhaps he wanted to think over what Paul said and pressure of work sidetracked him or perhaps he attributed the fear that had come upon him to some psychological malady—we don't know. We *do* know that Felix let his chance go and became so hardened as he listened to the Word of God from then on that he only listened because he hoped to find some financial gain in it. As far as we know from the Bible, the Word of God did not cause Felix to tremble at the second time of hearing—the chance never came again.

The rich young ruler met with Christ and we are told 'He went away sorrowful'—we do not read that he ever met with Christ again! The moment had passed and, as far as we know from Bible narrative, his chance of eternal salvation passed with the moment.

There never will be a more convenient time than now!

Felix said that he would hear Paul at a more convenient time but, as I have said, that more convenient time did not come.

There is a time in people's lives when they consider themselves to be too young to worry about the things of God—a little later perhaps! Then they are into their student days and there's so much going on there's not a lot of time to think about religion—perhaps when they have completed their studies! On the threshold of their careers they reason that it will be more 'convenient' to think of matters spiritual when they have established themselves. Then the girl of their dreams arrives and marriage is in prospect, and that, they reason, is most certainly not the right time to be thinking of one's eternal destiny! Then the children come along and life is taken up looking after them—but perhaps when the children have grown up it will be a convenient time! The children grow up and there is 'freedom' at last, it's time to enjoy oneself, just time for a last fling—then will be a more convenient time to think of religion! And so life flashes by until suddenly life's short day has passed.

No, there is no more convenient time than now!

We used to have question and answer sessions some years ago and the statement that 'Whosoever shall call upon the name of the Lord shall be saved' was guaranteed to bring forth one particular question.

'Can I not then,' would come the question, asked in that tone of voice which betrayed that the questioner thought himself or herself to be the first to have thought of it, 'call on my death bed?'

'Yes you can,' I would reply, 'but there are two conditions to be fulfilled before you can do that. Life in Christ is quite simply the best and most satisfying way of life one can have and so condition one is that you are prepared to *accept second best for the whole of your life.*' Then I would produce a piece of card and say, 'Even then there is some uncertainty about you being able to call upon the name of the Lord on your death bed but if you will fill in this card giving me the time, date and place of your death I will be able to tell you for sure if you can or not!' Back would come the reply, 'How do I know when I am going to die?'

You see the point don't you? If we knew exactly when we were going to have a fire or burglary in our house we wouldn't insure it for a year, we'd insure it for the day! It's precisely because we don't know what will happen to our house and when it will happen that we have to insure it all the time.

There are three reasons then why there is no time like the present. Firstly, there is no better way to live in the here-and-now, secondly, we do not know when we are going to pass into the there-and-then and thirdly, as with Felix, you may never be brought face to face with God again.

I have said that the Spirit of God often strives with a person for a very short time during their life. God calls that time 'the accepted time'. I know a man who at a time in his life, as with Felix, was convicted under the gospel message and, as King Agrippa, was almost persuaded to be a Christian but he waited for a more convenient time.

He was a strong healthy man at that time and

IT'S DECISION TIME!

remained so for some ten years after. Then he was taken ill and died after an illness lasting over a year. He had plenty of time for a death bed repentance but it didn't happen! This man who had been interested in spiritual things in the days of his health but had delayed doing anything about it, could not become interested in the final days of his life. Nothing that could be said to him seemed to register. That man had passed 'the accepted time', had had his chance and spurned it—the chance did not come again!

There are few more dangerous doctrines I think than that which maintains that the Spirit of God strives with men and women throughout the whole of their lives. In my experience it is far from the truth—there is very definitely 'an accepted time'.

I think of Pharaoh when Israel was in Egypt. Pharaoh had many chances but after the *first* chance to obey God, everything God did only had the effect of hardening Pharaoh's heart. As I have said, I don't understand it but I have seen this principle in operation time and time again.

The Spirit of God is working in your heart now but I wouldn't like to guarantee that He will be working in your heart tomorrow, or next year, or when you lie on your death bed—I don't know, neither does anyone else and nor do you!

'Now,' God says, 'is the accepted time, now is the day of salvation.'

I cannot overemphasise the need for you to make your decision now. As I have said, I have seen the tragedy of delay so often—men and women brought face to face with their eternal destiny, delaying a decision and the Spirit of God seemingly departing from them. Again I confess that I do not understand it but I have seen it! I remember when I began to learn the guitar, very unsuccessfully I might add, how sore the ends of my fingers and the fingers of the other students became. Weeks later my fingers were no longer sore, I could press the strings for hours without feeling any pain. Some of the students who, unlike me, persevered with the course later became professional guitarists and played hours each night six nights of the week without any discomfort. I think, perhaps, if the calling of God is not accepted when it is first given we 'get used to it' and it has no more effect on us.

What a tragedy to be approached by the Spirit of God and turn Him away!

God has spoken to *you*—don't turn a deaf ear because if you do you may never hear His voice again!